# SING ME THE SONG OF MY WORLD

FOR ALL THOSE IN THIS WORLD WHO SUFFER
AND HAVE NO HOPE

FOR ALL THOSE IN THIS WORLD WHO HOPE
AND SHARE THE LOT OF THOSE WHO SUFFER

Drutmar Cremer

# Sing me the Song of my World

*English adaptation by*
*Sister Benedict Davies, OSU*

**St Paul Publications**

Original title: *Sing mir das Lied meiner Erde*. Copyright © 1978 Echter Verlag, Würzburg. The translator is very grateful to the following and others for their advice and help: Sr Magdalen Bellasis, osu († 1980), Wesgate, England; The Ursuline Community of Salzburg, Austria.

The illustration on the cover represents a stained glass window, by Georges Braque, in the chapel of the Maeght Foundation in St Paul de Vence, in the south of France. For the photograph we are indebted to Toni Schneiders, Lindau © 1978 Copyright by ADAGP, Paris and Cosmopress, Geneva.

Acknowledgments are made to the undermentioned publishers for permission to quote from the following works:

*Hindu Scriptures*, translated by R. C. Zaehner, Everyman's Library Series, J. M. Dent & Sons Ltd. Copyright © 1966 and 1972.

*Longest Journey*, John Dalrymple, copyright © 1979, Darton, Longman & Todd.

*The Koran*, translated by and copyright © N. J. Dawood, 1956, 1959, 1966, 1968, 1974. (Penguin Classics, Fourth revised edition, 1974). Reprinted by permission of Penguin Books Ltd.

*Westminster Hymnal*, hymn text, 'Sower and seed' by R. A. Knox, Search Press.

**St Paul Publications**
Middlegreen, Slough SL3 6BT

English translation © St Paul Publications 1981
First published in Great Britain October 1981
Printed by the Society of St Paul, Slough

ISBN 0 85439 191 6

*St Paul Publications is an activity of the priests and brothers of the Society of St Paul who promote the christian message through the mass media.*

# PREFACE

Where can we find salvation today? When all is darkness and we are overwhelmed by modern systems of thought, what can bring our restless hearts a glimmer of hope? Is industrial prosperity the only valid answer for everyone? Does not belief in seemingly unlimited technical progress amount to superstition?

East and West alike use prosperity, social justice and peace as indispensable keywords in their propaganda. But are these concepts convincing and relevant for the millions who are suffering hunger and misery?

Optimistic forecasts for the future have grown noticeably more muted in recent years. We have become sceptical faced as we are by nuclear threats and the struggle for basic human rights.

We search for a deeper foundation to our lives and for a practical model, for one which rings true and is worthy of our confidence.

### SING ME THE SONG OF MY WORLD

— This title lures us beyond brash catchwords into the real depths of our lives, depths obscured by those wielding power in our times.

In this book Christians of different denominations, Jews, Mohammedans and Hindus from the most far-flung countries of the world pray that the Holy Spirit may transform us and our world. Letters, conversations and world-wide contacts have made the anthology possible. Thanks to an idea conceived by one of those helping the editor, numerous letters, like so many carrier-pigeons, were sent out on long journeys. Few remained unanswered. Most of the letters evoked a favourable response, testifying to faith in the power of the Spirit. Since some of the invitations were declined, more letters went out. The replies, many of which brought depressing news, laid stress on conditions prevailing in the world of today. One writer was unwilling, for fear of personal reprisals, to reveal his name. However, all who have written are aware of a new consciousness of their responsibility, as individuals, for each and all. In this "loveless age" they pray for an active love which sets aside as irrelevant power, political influence and material advantages. They pray without any idealistic emotion. Their observations are realistic, critical and accurate. They complain and they accuse. They sigh and weep for the painful, unfair burden laid on the shoulders of nations and on the hearts of men.

SING ME THE SONG OF MY WORLD

— These people pray because they have faith. They have faith in God's Spirit who is with them, giving them confidence in man's spiritual power to think, and to think in a new way. Their hope is nourished by the deep-rooted experience that God's Spirit can sing — using the lips of human beings — the "wonderful song" of our world. This love-song leads to unity and a friendly sympathy. It sets man free from endless pressures and anxieties because in his inmost being he is given "a new heart and a new spirit" (cf. Ez 36 : 26).

## Sing me the Song of my World

— This song arouses the mighty power of the Spirit and also the creative power of man. All the contributions to this "song of the Spirit" are, with one exception, original, and were written expressly for the book. The writers are at one in their belief in a more humane future under the inspiration of the Spirit. Only through the Spirit will the world rise up to become God's new earth. And man living on this new earth can suddenly raise his voice again and call out because he himself has been called. The book ends with the words: "I have a name for you. You are the crack of light under the door of the city morgue. Any minute now I may hear my name called: 'Lazarus' ".

Drutmar Cremer

---

After each prayer in this book we give the status or profession of each author and his native country, sometimes adding the country of residence.

I SHOULD LIKE TO FIND A WISE MAN
and share his life for a time,
read in his eyes, his hands, his world,
and I should like
to ask him questions:
— not the inquisitive questions asked by reporters,
who are mere outsiders,
but my own urgent, difficult questions
that have been with me since childhood:
What dream have you never ceased to dream?
Where would you be willing
once more to risk and lose your life?
What wounds in the heart of our world
wound your own heart?

I should like to find people and places
where not only the clever hold the floor,
explaining everything and showing off,
but where experienced people question,
people who are tolerant and open,
where the unimportant and the helpless
are allowed to tell of their wildest hopes,
uninhibited like children
whom one expects still to have their longings.

I should like to find time, energy and imagination
for my life,
and not be hounded, torn apart and manipulated,
before I learn to see the world and people
and to love their secrets.
I should like to meet those who feel concern,
compare their hopes with mine,
dare, with many others, to live out our times boldly
like a verse in the cosmic poem of God's Spirit,

that Spirit who, through us, renews the face of
    the earth
where and as and when he wills.


I have read much about you
whom people call God's Spirit:
in their experience and their reflections
they have found
lofty thoughts and daring symbols for you,
using intimate, delicate imagery.
These are enlightening and tell me much,
and if I go on asking questions and listen for long
    enough,
with sufficient simplicity and patience,
I can learn a great deal about you.
Yet I suspect
that I cannot find you
by accepting you in my life
as mere knowledge and thought.
I suspect that, in and through my life,
I must spell you out afresh,
that together we must find our words for you.
You are so mysteriously hidden
and so small and silent.
Woven into the very fibres of our being
you would wish to bring everything into play.
What were we thinking of
when we took our lives away from you,
when we removed you from our lives
and made you abstract — a mere idea?


But you did not take your life away from us —
you are God's long-drawn-out breath in us,
God's hope,
refusing to allow us to be crushed and fall apart,

God's love for us,
never letting us give up.

You remain steadfast in us
even if we don't remain steadfast,
you hope in us,
even if we no longer see sense in anything,
you think of us,
even if we think only of ourselves.

Are you the yearning in my love,
the surprise in my eyes,
the silent weeping in my wounded heart?
Are you with me in my questioning,
is your silence in my loneliness
the loneliness of God,
are you singing the melody of your heart
in the song of my world?
Are you God's smile in my tears,
God's trust in my anxiety,
God's suffering in my guilt?
We can extinguish your Spirit in us, Lord,
we can put to death your life in the world,
distort it and wall it up
until it is no longer recognisable,
but we cannot take from you
the glowing fire of your great love.
For it happened once
that your great love — and ours —
came to terms
when Jesus surrendered his life to you
and you surrendered yours to him.
His Spirit is yours
and your Spirit is lavished upon us.
Make us alive and active through you,

make us daring for you,
make our world new,
for it was and is and will be
a mystery of your love.

Theologian - Lecturer in Education / West Germany

I MET KOBER.
He gave me no greeting.
He cut me dead.
Does he really hate me?
I know he frowns
on many of my views
and my activities.
However:
I didn't make any effort to greet him.
I thought
I'll treat you as you treat me.
Why should I force myself upon you,
appear friendly and give you an artificial smile?

Lord,
it would be better if I didn't meet him again,
or as seldom as possible.
But suppose our paths do cross again?
Then at least let it be at a propitious moment,
when I'm in a good mood,
for you know well
what a moody man I am —
Therefore at the right time,
so that I have the desire
and the courage
to give him a greeting and a smile,
simply, naturally.
Then perhaps the coolness between us
might come to an end?
You've already put an end
to more awkward situations, haven't you?
Lord, I don't want to dictate conditions to you.
But if we had to meet again
I should be delighted if you could be there,
if you would touch me very gently

and give me courage
to break down the barriers.
Or manage it in whatever way you wish,
in me and through me,
Lord.

Lord,
I met Kober again.
Before I had time to think
I greeted him.
Suddenly he was there in front of me,
he had just rounded a street corner,
we almost collided
and, as we did so,
the greeting escaped me.
You arranged it very cleverly, Lord,
you really are artful and you have a heavenly sense
    of humour!
Later on I thought:
a leading inspiration from your Spirit
who is holy
because he can be so completely down-to-earth.

And what about Kober?
Alleluia! he returned my greeting.
A bit grumpily, but he greeted me.
Where did my sudden spontaneity come from?
You know well enough how diffident I am,
anything but spontaneous,
you seem to have outwitted me completely
and taken me by surprise.

And what a trifle it was!
Since the event I am dismayed,
I am ashamed I bothered you about it.

Lord,
I want to try not to call on you
for such trifles.
You have shown me now
how to take the first step:
why in future
shouldn't I take such steps alone,
I mean, manage to do so without you?
You would just have to help me
to loosen up
my timidity and my nervousness,
to give me courage for the spontaneity
born of your Spirit.
Then I think I can learn
to walk on my own two feet
towards Kober, towards others,
without needing you each time
to touch me, to urge and help me
with a special inspiration.
This would mean:
going forward in your peace,
my head held high,
as an advocate for the joy of life
and for the brotherly friendship of Jesus.
Yes, something of this kind.

Pastor - Poet / Switzerland

HOLY FATHER,
you have led us
into a land of sunshine.
The palm beaches of the Caribbean,
humid virgin forests,
the shimmering glow of sweeping plains,
the rich colours of the slopes of the Andes,
day in, day out, your sun sheds its rays
over them.


And in the midst of all this
you place us human beings,
the pride of creation,
like a jarring note in the symphony of life.
One child in every three
calls out for his unknown father.
The tin roof rattles
over eight bodies
asleep in their one-roomed hut.
And close by is the clinking of champagne glasses
at a tedious society cocktail party.


Your Son knocks gently
on the doors of the hearts
of all those baptised in his name.
If only young men and women
would guard their fecundity as a precious
responsibility,
if only those who should offer influence and wisdom
would be open-handed!
The gap which life has widened
must be acknowledged in faith as scandalous
and must be narrowed
by the combined efforts of our love.

You make our earth
so fruitful in oil and ore,
yet we should indeed all be poor
if our hearts were full
only of hard cash.
Keep us, Father,
in the happy life-style of our forefathers
and in fidelity to the guidance of the Church.
As oil flows from the ground
out to the whole world,
so may a stream of gratitude
rise in our hearts
and spread far and wide in your divine world.

Among us dwell blacks and whites,
American Indians and Japanese.
This friendly intermingling of all nations
in our country
might well be a hope
for the future of mankind.
But, Father,
the iron railings in front of every house
imply that our hearts
have not yet found a place of rest.
Lord Jesus!
May your Spirit penetrate
our stubbornness.
May your will, not our self-will,
prevail in us,
for this land of sunshine will pass away
and you alone will lead us all to our homeland,
to your Father and our Father.

Teacher / Venezuela

B

ALMIGHTY GOD,
you sent your Son to us
to offer his life
for our sins
and lead us
to peace, reconciliation and love.

After two thousand years
we fall far short
of living according to your will.

In some countries
we allow ourselves
to be dominated
by mental sloth and apathy.
We forget our suffering brethren,
and, in so doing, we forget Jesus Christ
and his cross.

In other countries
we allow ourselves
to be threatened by physical violence
and driven to lies and hypocrisy,
we set ourselves against you and your truth
and adore the brute beast and its image.
Often through fear
even our pastors dissemble
and lead us into the temptation
to betray you.

Is there any hope left for this world?
Not only your Son
but ordinary people too
have died for our sins,

to rouse us to action.
Jan Palach and Pastor Brüsewitz
feared our tepidity and sluggishness
more than the flames of death.
In many countries
brave people
run serious risks
when, full in the public eye,
they defend human rights and values
against the most deadly despotism.
They are persecuted, slandered, imprisoned,
yet they do not abandon their struggle
for the Spirit
against violence.
There is the movement for human rights
in the Soviet Union,
the group "Charter 77"
in Czechoslovakia,
there are intellectuals and other brave men
in all countries behind the iron curtain,
— in the other part too of Germany.*
For all of us, in conscience,
this should be a challenge.
However, we are not — as yet — awake and alert.
We hardly deserve your help,
but we know that your mercy
is even greater than your justice.
You never allow us to succumb completely,
you strengthen us in temptation,
you do not let us drive you out of our lives —
not even
when in our stupidity and stubbornness
we attempt to do so.

* Written by someone living in West Germany

Individuals and whole nations
experience your love in these hard times.
We fall repeatedly
and you support us repeatedly.
When we are oppressed
you make us question in our hearts
the meaning of our life.

We thank you, dear Lord, that you do exist,
even though so many foolish people,
because they are too clever,
declare you dead.
We thank you for being the fulfilment
of our lives
and for giving them meaning.

There is hope — even for this world —
and we want
with all the ardent love of our hearts
to search for this hope.

We beg you
to give us strength and a spirit of sacrifice
which would lead us to work together
for unity and brotherly love.

We beg you
to make us weak when we feel too strong,
to admonish us when we go astray,
to give us courage when defence
of your truth is at stake.

We beg you
to strengthen our faith —
because it is not our reason

but our faith
that is the hope of the world —
There is hope even for this world.
We thank you,
merciful God,
for this hope!

International Chess Player - Journalist / Czechoslovakia -
West Germany

**LORD,**
there are many people in this world
who have known only suffering
in their lives.
Born in time of war,
war is all they know.
Wherever they go,
they see only ruins,
misery, anxiety, wounds and tears.

Millions of dead,
widows,
girls left all alone,
orphans, refugees.

Houses, schools, bridges,
factories, towns
destroyed!
Mothers abducted,
children carried off,
men tortured,
women beaten.

Lord, there is no end to this injustice!
Enormous sums of money
are squandered on arms.
The rich live in luxury.
Many people are out of work.

A Vietnamese poet has said:
"God, if man is made in your image,
then your image is being torn apart".

O Lord, you know
the gravity of the distress.

Our society has need of you
and our Church has even greater need of you.
We need your light
and your help
to overcome
our selfishness and our helplessness.

Lord, without your light and your strength
we cannot renew the world.

The light of the gospel
does not as yet shine everywhere.
Our society is godless.

It is good, Lord,
that from bitter experience we know our helplessness,
for in this way
we shall be able
to find our way back to you.
Lord, send down your Spirit.
Through the light and strength of your gospel
renew our society.

Theologian / North Vietnam - West Germany

## MY ROOTS BURN

in hollow place
below rocking water. Fire
eating ice
draw me
deeper
down.

You slip through my soul
wisp of wind
wandering on
when I want to hold you. Within
the world's time, inside
its élan
you hide.
The poor know
you care, you are there
when we come.

Sing to us
Spirit of God.

Trappist - Poet / USA

ONLY YESTERDAY
we gave them work and bread,
Lord,
those two young blacks.

With my own hands
I prepared their meal
and waited on them.
We made their worries our own
and exchanged friendly words.
They played with our children.
Their laughter still re-echoes,
mingling with the children's squeals of delight.
My little girl was just beginning to walk.
Her golden curls gleamed in the sun.
Her baby sister smiled in her cradle,
her eyes shining like stars.

Dear Lord,
it happened this morning,
the feast of Saint Patrick.
As every day
my husband set out to visit you
at the early Mass.
It must have been your angel
who, before my husband set foot on the steps,
made him turn his head.
And there,
half-hidden behind the open door,
stood one of the blacks,
hatred and fear alike in his expression,
an enormous, heavy piece of iron
raised on high.
And then he struck.

How can I thank you,
dear Lord,
for giving my husband
the presence of mind
to slam the door in his face
with all his might and main?
The heavy steel door had caught
the full force of the blow,
only chin and shoulder were hit.


The other black
had been lurking in ambush,
hidden at the bottom of the steps,
pick-axe in hand.
In the narrow space
between house, garage and workshop
my husband would not have stood a chance.
Dear Lord,
I shudder
to think of what might have happened . . .


The little girl had crept into my bed early that
        morning,
the baby lay in her cradle,
both fast asleep.
Still weak after a difficult birth
I was saying my morning prayers.
As you know, Lord,
I go to a later Mass with the children.
Suppose they had killed us too,
or, as one so often hears,
tortured us for hours on end
before disappearing
with our car laden to capacity?

Dear Mother Mary, thank you
for spreading your mantle over us!

When my husband,
pistol in hand, ready to fire,
saw them running away like frightened rabbits,
why didn't he shoot them?
Dear Lord,
it would have been easy for him to do so.
He says he thought of their mother.
In pain she had given birth to her sons
and with great difficulty she had brought them up.
She loves her children
as we love ours
and as our mothers love us.
And yet, Lord,
tomorrow those two young blacks
will murder others —
whites, blacks, Indians, Chinese, half-castes . . .

The devil knows
no distinction of races,
nor do his red henchmen
who have misled these two young men
with lies and false promises.
And yet the West looks on.
And your Church?
What is she doing?

Here on my knees,
Jesus,
before you shining in the monstrance,
I pray,
Lord, have pity on your world.

Give us and our children
your peace.
Penetrate the world and transform it,
Holy Spirit, firebrand of love.
Amen.

Philosopher / Austria - South Africa

IN THE TULIP TREE
in front of my window
is perched a woodpecker.
The sound it makes
is that of hard blows
chipping away
with muffled rhythm
at the firm wood.

In like manner
dreams press in upon me,
involuntarily, ever returning;
pictures are formed in my mind,
flashing like sheet-lightning,
circling silently and fleetingly
in my inner self;
a self that I have long searched for —
as unconcerned as a child —
a self that every human being
hopes one day to discover
hidden under the shelter of his own wings:
a new Paradise brilliantly lit,
but not the paradise of every supermarket with
    its wares,
one that meets every material need,
while never able to satisfy the questions of our hearts.

In like manner
your Spirit knocks
ceaselessly, firmly,
untiringly, coming back again and again.
It breaks open the outer shell
and thrusts its way into the inmost depths
where harmony can grow out of discord:
where, freed from anxiety and the drudgery of life,

renewed,
brothers can meet once more;
where nations,
as if guided by a sure hand,
can come together
around the "tree of life".

The fruit of this tree
is not progress
lacking centre and proportion,
gained at the cost
of those who dwell chiefly in southern countries,
peoples whose misery, hunger and despair
threaten to change into hatred and rebellion
whence there is no way out.

The fruit of the tree
provides fresh insight,
giving to the finest among us
a quiet strength for sharing,
so that the peoples of this world
may be reconciled and cease to fight,
and so that the wealth of this earth
may be at the service of everyone,
not only of the rich —
they see an endless amount of fruit
but they can never harvest
the "fruit of life".

The fruit of the tree
nourishes the strong too,
those who, in the turmoil of their hectic enterprises,
in the heavy demands they make on their own lives,
think first and foremost of their achievements and
     their gain.
It nourishes the weak,

the poor and the aged,
inviting man
to celebrate his dignity as man.
Despite affliction,
anxiety and doubt,
he can at every moment live
in the assurance that he is loved.

The fruit of the tree
gives strength to dream
of forming the "new world",
a world destined to have a future
that will never pass away.

The fruit of the tree —
is the fruit of the Spirit.
It is the 'yes' of eternal importance
and the fruit of the sacrifice
that breaks through all times and frontiers.
How can fruit be brought forth without death? —
When dark sorrow comes upon me,
because perhaps in today's struggle
I can no longer believe
in the freedom promised for tomorrow,
and when sadness casts its long shadow over me,
in the ray of light
you yourself have created,
beyond the poison of those clouds from Seveso,
I contemplate
the Father's hand
bringing peace
and a voice
which, moved by tongues of fire, calls:
I say: Get up and walk!

Benedictine Monk / West Germany

## SALUTIS HUMANAE SATOR

"Sower and seed of man's reprieving"—*
By this majestic imagery
the words of the ancient Latin hymn
help me to pray
to you, Jesus,
as you ascend to heaven
that you may scatter,
as good seed,
wherever you will,
your Spirit
in his gifts without measure.
As long as we belong to the earth,
an earth ready to accept these gifts,
we are empowered to produce your fruit,
empowered through your Spirit
to let your Word be born anew,
to give new birth for the world to your Word,
ourselves to be for that world your living word.

In this hymn
I am always left
with a question
to ask of you, Lord.
May I ask it?
Or is it the wrong question?—

And yet it would seem to me to touch the innermost
        depths of your heart:
"Qua victus es clementia,
ut nostra ferres crimina?"
"What sovereign pity earthward drew thee,
our load of sins thy charge to make?"*
You are the Lord, you are the Son,
God from God

* Translation from *Westminster Hymnal*, N. 60, Search Press.

and Light from Light.
"Behind" you and "above" you
there is nothing,
you are the pure, clear utterance of the Father.
And yet here it is stated
that there would seem to be something stronger
    than you,
and clearly stronger too than the Father,
certainly stronger
than anything we can imagine
when we speak of your Godhead and his,
of your personal power and his.
It is the power of goodness, gentleness,
by which you are carried away
and will to become wholly and completely one of us,
will to let our burden become yours,
to leap over the intervening distance
and come to the farthest bounds
and there bear the full weight of the world
with the whole of its history.
There can indeed be nothing greater,
nothing higher than you,
nothing prior to you.
What comes upon you
and carries you away
is your very self, the depths of your being.
God is love,
so this means
that love is more than God,
than what we imagine as God,
love,
boundless, gratuitous love
is the "first and earliest" thing about God,
you yourself are the Word,
the pure utterance of such love.

You look upon the Father and see
that He loves only you,
but in so doing, and for that very reason,
He loves all of us, the whole world.

And so your gaze passes,
while still riveted on the Father,
beyond Him
and you turn with Him towards us, towards the
    world,
towards what is not God,
yes, even towards what is against God.
You accept this rejection
and transform it
into what you and the Father are,
into love.
This is the love
which you give to one another,
and which you give to us:
the Spirit of the Father.
Love which also makes us human,
vulnerable and defenceless,
enrapturing and enraptured,
so that we can give ourselves
as you are given.
This is the seed
which, as you pour out your Spirit,
you give us in our hearts,
this is the Word
which we, through the Spirit,
should become in our flesh.
Yes, Lord, give us this Spirit
which drives us into your heart,
making us look only at you
and exist only for you —

and it is precisely this that drives us,
beyond you, with you,
with you into the world,
to be there with you,
where, in the uttermost limits of obedience and love,
you said your 'yes',
your 'yes' to the Father
and to Him alone
unconditionally —
and for that very reason
your 'yes' to us, just as we are
and wherever we are.

And so we make the selfsame petition:
take us,
"Sower and seed of man's reprieving",
with you to the Father's heart
and cast us into it and thus
straight into the heart of the world!

Theologian / West Germany

## WHERE HAVE THEY GONE,
those South American Indians
who dwelt among the tall pillars of their virgin
    forests,
who, in earlier times, were the guardians
of rivers, trees and animals?

Their tracks can still be followed.
The echo of their voices
has not yet died away.
But it is only rarely now
that the sun silhouettes their shadows.
Where have they gone?
They have been sacrificed to our "new era".

Their death struggle has been long drawn out,
they have been persecuted, killed and imprisoned,
dragged off to camps
and made slaves.
Was this in the interests of progress?
Deprived of their future and their past,
they were promised
— in your name, Lord —
integration and prosperity.
Instead of this they came to know
anxiety, misery and hunger.
Sickness and death
are their constant companions.
Wasn't this too high a price to pay for progress?

Now they have clearly come to terms with their lot.
Calmly, steadfast in faith,
they sing of their own downfall.

Their path, like that of a bird,
traces an ascending line.

They regard the white man as a tiger
that mercilessly tears their bodies to pieces.
Yet now, as in earlier times, they remain proud
    hunters.

Some of them are still alive
and there is still time to help
our brothers — for that is what they are —
to follow the road of life together,
and in peace.
This road brings deliverance,
freedom, life without end.

Historian / Paraguay - West Germany

## WHEN I WAS A CHILD
my eyes contemplated the traces you had left
in the shape and strength of a motionless stone,
in a solitary pillar from a ruined temple,
in the face of a god
emerging from the depths
of ancient, immovable rock,
delicately poised and held
over the abyss of timeless ages.

Silently the spirit blossoms in the vision of
      mythology;
I became vividly aware of the source of his words
above the cavern of images.
As he descends he dispels the darkness
without disturbing its primeval depths.

Only later did I comprehend
what the spirits were saying to each other.
On the lonely shores, the distant horizons where
      they dwell,
time like a string of pearls lies shattered.
The sound of their voices
loosens fragments from the mountain of knowledge
that is forever beyond our ken.
As a wind-blown compass
the voices form and direct our thoughts.

Plato and Augustine,
the dark night of John of the Cross,
the hallowed vision of mystic love,
Kierkegaard and the towering structure of Hegel's
      thought
are forces that hold back a void,
signposts set up by men above a chaos of nothingness.

Yet I saw:
thoughts like lofty trees
rising above a grey-black wilderness.
Into rivers beyond the future
are dropped nets,
the songs of those
who perish here.

Of suffering too
an articulate remnant still remains.
Not only the throng of the spirits,
but also that of the sufferers,
those who died in concentration camps and
    fratricidal wars
— and every war is waged against brothers —
those who, wide-eyed,
hold out the empty bowl of their hunger,
all these appeal for witnesses of this suffering.
From the depths of time
they ask for more than the mute appeal
of eye and eye-lid carved in stone.

However, I am waiting and hoping:
speak your word once more over clay and dust,
over the empty, restless core of our existence,
over the compass void of all direction
of our self-opinionated knowledge,
over our daydreams and tongue-tied silence,
over our hearts grown hard,
over the poverty of our hands,
speak the word, the one word,
that sets us free.

Writer - Mother of a family / West Germany - Spain

## GOD

created the races
with differences
of form and skin.

But he did not create
hatred.
This was spread far and wide
by man's foolish errors
when he turned aside from the path of Scripture
where there is no mention
of hatred between races.

Even if the human eye has been inclined
to see other differences,
the true Spirit of God
is aware of none.

Common to all races
is a striving for happiness
and freedom from the limitations of our world.

Lord, your Church
was the first to understand
that the strongest bond
uniting the races of the world
is the longing for freedom.

So your Church has spread abroad
among all men
love and solidarity.
Your disciples, your missionaries,
were the first to intermingle
with other nations
and give to young and old
their knowledge
and the message of salvation.

They were the first to proclaim
that compassion and sympathy
for our neighbour,
for our brother in Africa,
and our sister in Asia,
do more to unite us all
than skins of different colours
can ever do to separate us.
Your disciples
did not shrink from trouble and hardship,
even persecution,
in order that your message of freedom
might spread and take root.

And so today too
it is more important than ever before
that in all parts of the world,
in desert, jungle and steppe,
your Church
should not grow weary
of struggling and suffering
for fellowship and peace
among the races,
so that obsession, prejudice and hatred
among the races
may finally come to an end.
Lord, this is the petition we make to you.

Dentist / Indonesia - West Germany

## O MY GOD
I look to you for help.
For I have no strength.
I need your help,
my body is weak and sickly.

My soul is even weaker;
Lord, I have no courage.
You are far from me,
I feel useless,
I am all alone.
What I have done for your people
seems worthless,
I have wasted my time.

Strengthen my spirit,
restore to me my former energy,
give me your strength.
For how am I to think of you
if I see only misery
and feel I have achieved nothing.

How am I to praise you
if continually I think death is coming
and still see no fruits for my labours.

I am exhausted
from crossing rivers,
from talking without being listened to,
from wounds on my feet,
from danger
and from working late into the night.

At night I think
that my day has been wasted,

the next day brings fresh fatigue;
I feel that the years are passing
and that my neighbours and those around me
scoff at me.

Keep these thoughts far from me:
I know you listen to me
and accept my prayer.

With you I will continue the struggle;
Lord, I will put aside my doubts,
for I believe you are near me.
Do not leave me alone and do not allow me
to depart from your presence
and your people.

Theologian / Columbia

LORD,
daily we meet people
in our streets,
our homes, schools, offices,
workshops and churches . . .
and again and again I penetrate more deeply
into the mystery of life
which in countless ways
is ever being renewed in man.

Before my eyes
is a long line of the mysteries
of birth and death,
the courageous daring of youth
and the helplessness of old age,
the cheerfulness of the healthy
and the hard struggle of the sick,
the resentment of the godless
and the anxiety of humble,
neglected believers,
the mystery surrounding man's work,
his skill and his success,
the mystery of those who have bartered away
    their souls,
the homeless, the unemployed . . .

Lord,
I am wholeheartedly steeped
in the mystery of human life,
in the great drama of our puzzling days.
My brothers,
sold in foreign markets,
live in my heart,
their children left behind,
lonely widows seated in front of a hearth

where no fire burns,
all the building sites and workshops
— temples of the proletariat.
My heart bleeds for hundreds
of lives lost, frightened, crushed.
I am haunted by the faces
of the passers-by
on the pavements of my city,
and the musty smell
of the dreary barracks in our suburbs.
I am in anguish
for those out of work and those made redundant,
I feel in myself the fate
of those brave intellectuals now persecuted,
in me is the blood of my faithful Croatians
dedicated thirteen long centuries ago,
in me lives the powerlessness of my Church,
the re-echo of all her trials and tribulations . . .

Lord,
is this all an endless drama of destiny,
or the sacrifice of life itself
on the altar of unknown gods,
are we helplessly sacrificed
to the God who has no meaning?

Lord,
I believe in your Spirit
dwelling in silence
in the depths of our soul,
in the heart of this our world
and in the whole of our lives.
I believe in the Spirit
who sets us free from our lack of freedom,
transforming our infidelity into faith,

giving meaning to our meaningless days
and transforming
our blasphemous curses into prayer.
I believe in the Spirit
who gives firm support to all our sufferings
transforming
into a new heaven and a new earth
each atom of our mother-earth,
at whose breast
we drink the milk of our own damnation,
that Spirit who transforms
into a magnificent eternity
the brief span of our earthly days.

Lord,
your Spirit hovers over us
and your sun does not obscure our hopes,
nor can our nights
prevail against the strength of your day,
and our hearts cannot remain closed . . .
Your Spirit, O God, treads
our winding paths.
It calls and delivers us
from our daily shortcomings;
softly it whispers to us in the twinkling of the stars,
gently it smiles on us in the eyes of every child,
in a loving word from our dear mothers,
in the little joys of our earthly days,
in a letter from a friend,
a meeting with someone we know,
the loyalty of a friend . . .

Lord,
through the power of your Spirit in me
I believe that the mystery of our life

is not unfathomable,
that our anxieties are not justified,
that the questions we ask
are not without an answer,
that human life is not just an accumulation
of pain and misery.

O God,
you are always with us, for us, in us.
You are our God and Father
even when we say that you are
absent,
non-existent,
inexpressible,
unknown . . .
You are, and always will be with us,
do not take your Spirit from us,
for without you, O God,
man would be condemned
to misery and damnation,
he would be without redemption,
without a redeemer . . .

Lord,
save each and every man,
save contemporary man.
Lord, thank you for saving man.
Amen. Amen.

Theologian / Yugoslavia

## ABEL, RISE UP,
we must act it out again,
every day we must act it out again,
every day we must be confronted by the answer,
it must be possible for the answer to be 'yes'.

Abel, if you do not rise up,
how can the answer,
the one and only important answer,
ever change?
We can close all the churches
and do away with all the statute books
in every language in the world
if only you rise up
and undo the first false answer
to the only question at stake.

Rise up,
so that Cain says,
so that he can say:
I am your keeper,
brother.
How can I not be your keeper?
Every day rise up
so that we are confronted by the answer:
Yes, I am here,
I, your brother,
so that Abel's children
need no longer be afraid,
because Cain is not going to be Cain.
I write this,
I, one of Abel's children,
and every day I fear the answer;
I am breathless with anxiety
as I wait for the answer.

Abel, rise up,
so that among us
things may be different.

The fires that burn,
the fire that burns on the earth,
is said to be Abel's fire.

And the fire in the tail of the rocket
is said to be Abel's fire.

Poet / West Germany

## DEAR JESUS,

Please try to teach us
in Northern Ireland —
the true love of you
and the words you left us all
to abide by:
My peace I leave you,
my peace I give unto you.

Help me be strong
and do the work set out by you.
Sometimes it is hard
and I don't understand,
sometimes I want to give up
when I hear of another horrible death
or one more terrible bomb.
Through you, with you, in you,
let me please do your work.
You suffered the most horrific death
before people realised
what you were all about.
People here have crucified you
over and over again
and sometimes have asked you
to cross your divine legs
as they have only one more nail left.

Help us and please forgive us
for what we have done.
You rose again from the dead today.
Guide us through this awful war
and help us to help you.
All our love, dear Jesus,
from the people of Northern Ireland.

Nobel Prize Winner / Northern Ireland

I AM A JEW
I find it hard
to pray to you in German.*
I pray that Germans
may grasp the grandeur of the Hebrew language,
the language of your first revelation.

You drive us out for victory.
You send us into exile
from our native land,
to disgrace, exploitation,
oppression, ridicule and mockery,
derision, sickness, loneliness,
coldness on the part of our loved ones,
suffering even for the cause of victory.
Everything that we your children suffer today
    so deeply
we suffer for victory.
The children of God
actually think in Hebrew
even if they do not understand it.
"Deep suffering"
and "suffering for victory"
are for us one and the same thing.

God, I know
that you gain nothing from my suffering.
Why then do you send me suffering?
I believe you send it
because it can become an enrichment for me.
You created
warm spring, hot summer,
gentle autumn, bitter, cold winter,
for our good.

* This prayer was written in German

You are one,
and everything created by you
is in harmony.
I have no eye for differences,
not even the difference
between joy and sorrow.
Blessed be everything,
for it all leads to victory.
You give each of us his cross
and you offer us the gift
of garlanding the cross with roses.
Then it becomes an ornament.

We think of the martyrs
in Communist and Moslem countries.
We thank you for the flowers of patience,
of love and heroism,
which we can gather from their crosses.

Make us aware
that our suffering
serves the cause of victory
and also of stillness.
The beauty of your son,
our Lord Jesus Christ,
is mirrored
only in still waters.
Only stillness can delight
one who is searching for stillness.
May we be like the fir-trees:
evergreen.
Help us, Lord, we beg of you. Amen.

Theologian / Rumania - USA

O LORD OUR GOD,
you have given us the name of Christian.
From you we have received the mission
to live in the world as Christians.
We have to live in this world
among people whose thinking is different from ours.
We have received the mission
to be Christians
in this kind of world,
one which regards us
and Christianity and religion
as a superfluous remnant.

Since Jesus did not pray
that you would take us out of the world,
neither do we pray
for circumstances to be changed.
We pray only for a real change in ourselves,
that we may be moulded into the likeness of Christ
and become worthy of his name.

We pray that here, in this new, changing world,
where words offering a solution to the problems of
    the human race
have to be proclaimed,
in a world that respects the paramount value of
    human beings,
we may be able to impart to men
true human kindness.
You have Good News for this world.
To all mankind you give the greatest gifts
of human kindness and of peace.

Give us the grace to experience this
and enable us to make it meaningful

for the young people
entrusted to us.

Help us in this world
— a world unwilling to recognise any God —
to pass on your love to everyone,
the love which forms man,
calls him into life,
invigorates and renews him.

If we greet only those
who greet us and are concerned for those
who are concerned for us,
if we can say a kind word
only to those who think as we do,
then as yet we are no sign
of your love . . .
Help us to recognise
our brother, "one of the least of these",
even in the unbeliever,
even in the one who is still searching,
in all those whose convictions
are different from our own.
Our chief aim should be
not that we may be understood.
What we need much more is a listening ear
and an open heart.
We must not crave for approval from our friends,
but rather extend to all
a kindly, helping hand
even if many of them say:
"Don't have anything to do with them".
May we be in this world
living signs of your love!
And if we have to teach in school

the young born into this world,
may we pass on with conviction:
"If we knew all mysteries,
had all insight and knowledge",
— if we can give no proof
of sincere human kindness,
we are nothing.

Lord, we thank you
for teaching us how to lead
a life like this,
a life where
we no longer have "silver and gold".
If all of us
whom you call to your service here
could declare with infectious enthusiasm
to each one born into this world
ignorant of you,
but waiting, lamed and helpless, for happiness:
"Silver and gold we have none,
but what we have we give you:
In the name of Jesus of Nazareth
get up and walk!"
This is the prayer we make to you — today.

Benedictine Monk / Hungary

MY GOD,
perhaps it is all quite simple,
perhaps the endless distress in this world
comes from the fact that we no longer
do what is straightforward, what is necessary:
listen, just listen
to the Spirit
which breathes where it wills,
just show that we are in earnest
about our faith,
that you are the Lord.
Then it would be clear
that it is our way, not yours,
that we have to question.
We, free by nature,
set free by you too,
so that, as people set free,
we may find you again.
Free —
not from fetters,
not from trouble,
sickness, sin —
yet free:
to say 'yes' or 'no'
to the Spirit
that breathes where it wills.

God, let this Spirit breathe
where we need to understand anew
that you do not have to render account to us,
but we to you.
Let us then understand
how straightforward everything is:
you are the Lord, your will be done, Amen.

Biologist / West Germany

LORD,
we, men and women of the Andes,
pray insistently to you
about the extreme poverty
in which we live:
we are abandoned
to the whims of nature
and still more to oppression
suffered at the hands of our fellowmen.

For centuries
we have suffered
in patient resignation,
contemplating your Son's bitter passion,
image of our pain,
caused by lack of nourishment,
lack of possible employment
for many of our young people
who are left,
faced only with abject poverty
or crime.
For there is no future
in plots of ground
drained by centuries of tillage,
because the fruits of our labours,
both in agriculture and mining
are taken advantage of by others,
who leave behind for us only a few crumbs.

We, men and women of the Andes,
obliged by sheer necessity,
have worked since our earliest childhood,
and this rough life leaves no time for play.

Yet, in spite of everything,
we know

that you are the God of mercy,
and you take pity on those suffering want.
So we come back to you
and pray insistently to you
from the depths of our hearts
— often in silence
like Mary at the foot of the cross —
to adore your divine providence
and to strengthen our hope
in a more humane brotherhood of man,
as you, Christ, teach us,
and as we practise
by generous hospitality.

Bishop / Peru

# A BLESSING, GREETING TO THOSE WHO PRAY!

May you be praised,
All-glorious One, our only Lord,
Fountain of light, Creator of darkness!
Giver of peace, all is of your making!
May you be praised,
you to whom we owe
our human nature, our earth and its final goal.

May you be praised,
you to whom thanks are due,
you who are near us
and take pity on our miseries.
May you be praised
for blessing us
and for granting us the grace
to work in your kingdom
and to share in its sufferings.

All-glorious One,
they flee before you
and adore idols
that only fade away.
Those who go astray are not yet mature —
they lack courage for the freedom
that you offer them.
Since they seek refuge in sickness,
away from your healing Spirit,
they are left with
nothing but pleasure and emptiness,
despair and war.
For these precocious childish folk
the God of their childhood is dead
and they no longer remember him.

And since you do exist,
you seem to them frightening,
you who melt our stubbornness,
who mould and purify us.

O man, child of the Most High,
pride of creation:
do you hear, are you listening
to the painful groaning of deep humiliation,
the oppressed cry of despair,
the ghastly impact of bombs,
the moans of those being tortured,
the gasps of those being choked,
the screams of animals in agony
being dissected to manufacture cosmetics.
You can't bear it
and you stop your ears;
be strong, listen,
listen to the cries of our misery.

Listen,
listen deep within yourself:
Satanic mills grind in you.
Not only from without does the sun
of war-industry, the anti-sun,
send its dark rays
into the house, into the garden
of helpless slaves:
it sheds its rays in you, yes, in you,
for in you and in me there is grinding,
rumbling, screeching, trembling, shivering.
Listen with your whole being!
Do not close your heart, be strong,
bear to listen
to the outcry in the depths of your being!

What wild clamours are heard,
deceptive whistling,
abominable atrocities,
the hissing of envy and hatred,
and from the distance clashing of drums
louder and louder:
the drummers are coming!
The legion of skeletons
is drumming mercilessly in us,
it rumbles, threatens, crushes us from within . . .

And now calm down,
feel in your breathing
the even rhythmical winnowing
of an angel within you . . .
sense the gentle wafting breeze —
like the Spirit of the Most High.

Our will is to praise you,
you who were, who are and who are to come;
our will is to hate no one,
except the evil in ourselves,
and to plead for the nations,
those most closely bound to us,
to be responsible, each for all,
each for his brother,
so that the earth may become yours!

We forgive those
who have grievously sinned against us
so that we may, Father,
again ask for your forgiveness.
May you be praised
for leading us out of temptation towards holiness.
Self-seeking brings death,

but you are the one who raises us from the dead.
May you be praised, All-glorious One,
you who give new life to Israel!
You whose Spirit breathes where it wills:
it strengthens
in all men of goodwill on earth
the desire to love,
it will uphold them through deepest darkness.

O man,
support your brothers in need,
set prisoners free,
keep faith with those who sleep in death.
Yes, to you we solemnly pledge ourselves,
your call spans the vault of heaven.

Architect - Town Planner / Austria - Israel

## YOUR LIGHT SHINES FOR ME

on days that become
ever shorter,
ever colder,
in the days and years
of my life.
In my despondency,
in my aversion
for people
who are so merciless,
so self-seeking,
so apathetic,
in all the listlessness
which grows in me
from day to day —
you are my light.
You are witness to the fact
that a person can be noble
selfless, kind,
friendly and lovable.
In my resignation
face to face with myself,
resignation which grows with the years,
in the conviction
that I am still
capable only of self-seeking,
you are my hope
of bracing myself
for greatness and goodness.
The darker and colder
my years become,
the more I need your light
to be able
to go on living as a person.

Chaplain to Students / Poland

## GOD, MAKE ME SENSITIVE
to the touch of your Spirit
of truth and goodness
on this dark earth!

I see too much
of conflict and suffering,
of suffering that is endless.
What does it mean?

God, make me sensitive
to the hidden work
of the Spirit,
work threatened and betrayed,
betrayed by me too.

Make me sensitive
to all that is human in man,
near me and far away from me:
mentally sensitive.

Make people sensitive
so that they see what they are doing,
where their paths are leading them
and what will become of their lives.

O God, I am greatly troubled
about this world, about mankind.
The riddles are too deep for me,
the questions too vast.

Yet I will not doubt,
will not and cannot doubt
if I become sensitive
to what is greater

than all riddles and questions,
all anguish and distress:
the wonder of our being,
the wonder of love and goodness,
of peace and hope,
the wonder of the Spirit.

God, make me sensitive!

Theologian / Norway

E

**LORD,**
your word still counts for too little with us,
the teaching of Confucius still prevails.
His ethics and moral teaching was and is our rule
of life:
we had no need to think for ourselves,
we had no need to organise our lives,
to see, to judge,
we had no need to act for ourselves.
Everything was firmly laid down on clearly-defined
lines.
We have learnt
to accept our tradition as it stands
and to imitate what is foreign just as it comes.
But you have created man
so that by virtue of his maturity
he can say 'yes' to you and to his fellowmen.

Lord, you created all men as your children,
as brothers and sisters.
You entrusted our neighbour to us
as a special responsibility.
Yet insufficient knowledge of our own selves
has made us equally blind to others.

Lord,
we long for your wisdom
which creates social justice for everyone
and demands of everyone
creativity, social commitment
and love for our neighbour.
Give to those who govern the good sense
which will enable them to establish
according to your ideas
just laws worthy of respect.

Give us all courage
to stand up for human rights.
Give us your inexhaustible strength,
give it especially to those who,
because they proclaim your truth,
suffer in prison:
priests, citizens, students, intellectuals.

Lord,
shield us from the "violence of oppression",
help us to make room
for justice and freedom
and, for your sake, to be able
to make them a reality
in this world of ours.

Social Worker / South Korea - West Germany

## THE LONGEST JOURNEY
is the journey
inward

— Dag Hammarskjold


I sit before you, Lord,
upright and relaxed,
with a straight spine,
allowing my weight
to descend vertically through my body
to the ground
on which I am sitting.

I fix my mind
within my body.
I resist that urge of my mind
to career out of the window
to every other place but this one,
and to career forwards and backwards in time
away from the present.
Gently and firmly
I keep my mind where my body is:
here, in this room.
In this present moment
I let go all plans, worries, anxieties.
I place them now in your hands, O Lord.
I release my grip on them
and allow you to take them over.
For the moment I leave them to you.
I wait on you,
passive and expectant.
You come towards me,
and I let you carry me.

I begin the journey inward.
I travel down inside me
to the inmost core of my being
where you dwell.
In this deep centre of my being
you are there before me,
ceaselessly creating and energising
my whole person.

You, God, are dynamic.
You are within me.
You are here.
You are now.
You are.

You are the ground of my being.
I let go.
I sink and merge into you.
You overwhelm me.
You flood my being.
You take me over completely.

I let my breathing
become this prayer of submission
to you.
My breathing,
in and out,
is the expression of my whole being.
I do it for you, with you, in you.
I have "become" you.
You have "become" me.
We breathe together.

And now I open my eyes
to see you

in the world of things and people.
I resume responsibility
for my future.
I take up again my plans,
worries, anxieties.
I grip the plough again,
but I know now
that your hand covers mine
and grips it over mine.
Renewed in strength
I go again on the journey
outward,
no longer alone,
but in partnership
with the Creator.

Theologian / Scotland

O MY MASTER
and Lord of the Universe,
I seek your protection
from the evil designs of Satan,
the avowed enemy of man,
and turn to you
for relief and redemption
from all that is foul,
ugly and unclean.

I know
that there is a mystery
behind the veil
that shrouds the things of clay
I see outside me.
I also know
that my inner world
is enveloped
by all those thick and impenetrable walls
that keep my real self
hidden from my own sight.
But I also know
that the mystery
behind the veil of things outside me,
as also behind the things
as they appear to me
in my inner world,
is ultimately anchored
in the divine ground
whence they draw their nourishment.
It is my prayer
that I should be helped
to become cognizant
of my real position
in the scheme of things

and so see the things
as they are
and learn to value them
for what they are worth.

My life
and my time on earth
I know are not my own.
At best
they are the opportunities
which my situation
in the scheme of things
provides for me
to transcend the plateau
of my present level of consciousness
to reach a higher level of being.
The space
between what I supposedly am
and what I can in truth be
can only be traversed
by your grace.
To begin with,
I know
that I ought to have
the humility
to see through the illusion
that I myself am nothing,
since Thou alone art;
secondly, the model of man
I wish to place before myself
is that of the perfect man,
who is Mohammed,
the Prophet of Islam,
since he has been chosen by Thee
to serve

as the final means of communication
of a divine message
which is contained
in the Holy Book,
and finally
as a believer
I am commanded to live
the sort of life
that has been enjoined upon me
in light of the wisdom
contained in the Holy Book.

The ultimate truth is divine,
it is absolute;
and here, as elsewhere,
the true beginning
towards living the life of truth
can have its origin only in fear,
in awe and in resignation
at the altar
of the inscrutable will.
May I have the humility
to acknowledge my weaknesses
so as to be receptive
to the healing touch
of divine grace.
Deep down in myself
I am somehow aware
that if I am
at all to be rendered
a fit vehicle
for the divine grace
to flow into,
I have to pass
through the fire of love

and thus be purified
before I am able to recognise
the truth of things.

All truth is one,
even as all being is one;
my suffering arises
from the illusion
that at present I know myself
other than my real self.

Indeed, I become guilty
of being an idol-worshipper
if I were to ascribe
to what is only the partial manifestation
of the absolute,
the totality and integrity
of the absolute.

I must move
from the feeling of fear and awe
through the passage of love
in order to reach a higher level of being —
which level I cannot know at present.
But, as a believer,
I accept that it is the divine life
that I have to immerse myself into —
even as the dew-drop by slipping into the shining sea
becomes a part of it.

In the humble prayer
I voice forthwith
in this Tabernacle of Silence
I can only situate myself
in the terrain

called the human margin.
Left to my own resources
I am not qualified
to see things as they are,
if only because I don't have the eye
that you, O my God, have
to see the truth with.
Till such time
as the divine grace uplifts me
and frees me from the limitations
imposed on me by my human condition,
I must learn to cultivate
a sentiment of reverence —
yes, reverence for what is above me,
reverence for what is around me,
and reverence for what is below me.

Above me is the majesty
and grandeur
of the starry heavens
which the feeble powers of my reason
cannot comprehend;
around me is the empire
of environmental warp and woof
of the tradition
in which I am steeped
and in which I have to be nurtured
before I can myself make a contribution to it
by securing its transformation
in the light of the heavenly ideals
bestowed upon me.
Below me
are the silent graves of my ancestors
and as and when I tread
upon this dear earth of God,

I know
that this muddy vesture of decay of mine
that came from it
will some day return to it
and "be to its dust equal made".

Help me, Thou, O Lord,
to realise here below meaningfully
my true station and duties,
and thus enable me to do
that which might please you —
for I know somehow
that in whatever pleases you
lies my own fulfilment.

High-ranking official / Pakistan

## HOLY SPIRIT
who brooded over the dark waters,
and morning came:
I want to dedicate my breakfast to you.

Here we are,
and we are not beautiful,
we are not strong,
and nightmares interfere
with our compassion and hope
for the future.

But this table
where we know each other so well
and where we still want to have breakfast
together
is a sign of grace today and for ever,
and we bless you for the taste of morning,
for the new earth and heaven that are present
and take their place here together with us.
You make it possible,
you give us this good laughter
and share with us some very intimate words
from our Brother and Lord Jesus,
because nobody knows and loves Him
as you do.

Suddenly we are beautiful enough,
suddenly we are strong enough
to love one another
and to pass the bread and butter.

We lift our hands
like children who want to be lifted up
to Father

and we leave all our tools aside for a while
because we want to praise you in song
for the blessings of the morning
when we can look into the face of one
of your little brothers and sisters,
and there see the sun rise.

Poet - Journalist / Sweden

JESUS, SON OF MAN,
all I need over me
is the shroud of night;
in your kingdom
I need
neither province nor canton
nor the emptiness of a haughty palace,
but only a damp clod of earth
hollowed out like a cradle.

In your kingdom
I long to be like you, with you,
a crust, a mouthful offered to all
without distinction or segregation
or barriers; . . .
And yet, Lord Jesus, look,
I am the darkness of Ethiopian Africa.
What dawn will deign to appear on my horizon?
What sun — save your sun —
will lighten the blue immensity of my firmament?

I long to be
the simple earthenware pitcher
carried daily by a child
to the spring
to slake the thirst of the village folk.
Look:
I am choked up like an old bottle
plundered by termites.
But your hand will loosen the bottle-neck.
At dawn I shall be the fountain-head of your spring,
I shall gurgle from the rock cleft by Moses' staff;
over the old-age rim of the well of Sichem
I shall shed the light of the midday sun
and the virginal freshness of living water.

I cannot refuse your will
with its fatherly presence in me;
I cannot renounce your will
with its creation of sonship in me.
I am the crossroads of the world
and on me are the footsteps
of all tribes, peoples and nations;
on me is the dust shaken from their feet,
and their lengthening shadows,
and their brotherly hands
in your hand,
with my hand . . .

I am the frail child
unable to walk.
I thought my brothers would support my weakness,
but we are all fragile reeds that only bend,
and upon us falls the fury of the storms.
You are the upright trunk,
you are the oak-tree.
You are the unfailing strength of the human race.

Lord Jesus, let our footsteps tread in yours,
on the track where you walk,
leaning heavily
on you.
Let me be the grain of wheat
that does not cling to your hand,
but speeds in flight towards the harvest.
I will not be the dry gravel in the Sahara,
blown about by the barren sandstorm,
but the dense forest of the Congo and Gabon,
the jungle where the monsoon has breathed the
        Spirit of renewal
and the face of the earth has been recreated . . .

You said:
I have clothed you
with the radiance of my eyes,
like armour encasing you,
like a necklace of great beauty.
I have woven a delicate fringe
of all the faces of the world:
the Chinese, the Japanese, the Indians, the
    Malayans,
the white peoples of the west,
those who faithfully reflected my gaze,
those who sowed cockle in the furrows of my Africa;
and my people who once existed
but are now no more than a dream
in my three Americas, North, South and Central,
and my new, powerful, abundantly productive
    Americas:
my Africa too, inconspicuous, sombre,
clear only in its faith
and its centuries of waiting;
here is your own tribe,
like a rainbow
encircling my ecumenical horizon.

You said:
One day
I called the universe out of nothingness;
the little girl, Light,
was the first
to answer my call.
I love brightness.
I am the splendour before the dawn,
I love fire.
I love the flame dancing on the tip of every torch
and the tiny flickering of a candle.

F

. . . Do not hide my light in the dark night of the
    bushel.

You said:
Be the ocean of my fire
on the ruined face of the universe,
the ocean could not resist the call of your deep need,
and here I am, at your side,
with the flood-tide of my desire,
the desire to set all alight . . .

You said:
Be the song of the flame
in the voice of my brethren,
the pygmies of Ituri and Gabon,
for in their voices
I have placed the splendour of my sun:
"You are not a son of the night,
black as the soot in your smoky hut;
you are a son of the bright clear day . . .
No, you are not a son of the night!"

What is left for us?
A little poverty, a little hope,
the depths of our weakness, the immeasurable wealth
of our childish nature . . .
Perhaps also of that same nature
which opens the firmament
in the tremulous hands
of a Father lost and found . . .
Now the month of Nisan is here,
sealing us with the blood of the Lamb
that sets us free.
Now is the paschal hour and the cenacle is prepared;
now on the road to Emmaus is

— against all hope —
the encounter.
There are two of us,
then three,
and more, . . .
from elsewhere
and everywhere
to complete your stature,
and the spreading of your arms,
binding earth to heaven,
and completing the full measure of mankind
to the limits of the Oikoumenia.
We are here . . .
give us your Bread.

Jesuit / Cameroon

## TODAY

I read in the newspaper
that others are taking up arms
and we must defend ourselves against them.
In Soweto
black demonstrators have been arrested.
We condemn Apartheid.
A plane has crashed into the sea.
No one from our country is among the dead.

Tomorrow, I shall read the paper again:
the world will be no better.
What ought I to pray for?

We do not know what we ought to pray for,
what is fitting.
Today I heard
that a friend had been kidnapped.
Eight men carried him off at night
from his home
in a town in Latin America.
No one knows where he is now.
I can do nothing to help him.

But the Spirit
pleads for the saints
in God's own way.

Today I visited a friend.
He is ill and has to have an operation.
I did not know how to comfort him.
He comforted me
and himself.
He said:
the Spirit comes to the help of our weakness.

Today I listened to a Bach motet.
Whenever I hear it
I am heartened.
My perplexities have not vanished
my helplessness has not been removed.
I am none the wiser as to how I ought to pray
but I am confident that this is true:
The Spirit comes to the help of our weakness,
he himself pleads for us
with sighs too deep for words.

Teacher / East Germany

## WHEN YOU BEGAN WORK ON ME,

I thought I understood,
Lord.
I thought I understood you
and I thought I understood myself
and I thought I understood my vocation.

How well I imagined I could tell others
all about you, about myself
and about my vocation!
But the longer I travel the road of life,
the less I understand.
You shatter, one after another,
my ideas and images.
Everything fades away from me,
you fade away
and become more intangible and ineffable.
I fade away, am drained and parched,
all my reasons, justifications and arguments
fade away.

What remains is numbness and silence
and an inability to understand.
I have become detached
from all that made me secure.
I have abandoned it all
in a foolish recklessness of love.
And I have still got nowhere.
I grope in the night.
I roam around in empty space.
I feel my way in darkness,
clinging, as it were, to the invisible handrail
of your Son's fate.
In my weakness I eat
nothing but the dry bread of your word.

And yet:
Thank you for alluring me.
Hunger and thirst for you
are for me nourishment
that tastes more delicious
than any dish served at table.
And having no home for your sake
shelters me more securely
than any earthly home.

Thank you for helping me to keep going each day.
Even if I cannot see the path,
each step haltingly taken
has always led to a further step.

Trappist / West Germany

GOD,
I see things disconnected, side by side,
thoughts, ideas, proposals, plans.
I see these things brought together, arranged,
 organised,
I see everything functioning faultlessly.
But all to no purpose,
for the better the world functions
the more unbearable it becomes.
It is not success that keeps us alive,
nor possessions and all the security
we have devised.
None of us seems to be capable of doing more
than our insight dictates,
and of raising life
above its disconsolate state.

But if someone gives his shirt too,
when his coat would suffice,
if he goes two miles with you
when one would suffice,
then he is truly alive.

God, give me your Spirit,
let me do more
than others expect of me,
let me bear more suffering
than people inflict on me,
let me believe more
than I can ever imagine.

God, give us your Spirit!
give us life!

Benedictine Monk / Austria

## ALL-POWERFUL LORD, HAVE MERCY ON ME!

Creator, boundless in your pardon,
I repent of my sins, cleanse me from them,
restore to me the beauty of my earlier days.

To you I consecrate my power of understanding,
your gift to me;
may it pierce the heart of the truth
of your abundant mercy
for a sinner like me.

To you I offer my eyes
which contemplate your creatures:
may they throw light on the world
and make my way clear,
showing me the evil
which would make me stumble.

Take my ears that have listened to error:
may they henceforth be attentive to the truth,
so that, when the evil one tries to speak to me,
I may, by your grace, be deaf to his words.

The offering most pleasing to you
is a contrite heart full of sorrow
for the faults which, in error, we have committed,
for the follies with which the arch-enemy poisons us.

My heart is not whole:
it is grievously torn,
it is crushed by sorrow:
take it into your care,
weld it together again
and keep it for yourself.

Make of it henceforth a radiant palace
where I may ceaselessly adore you,
returning to you the glory
that I stole when I went astray.
From the throne of your glory
forgive my sins, I pray:
those public faults known to all,
those which have given grievous offence,
as well as my most secret sins.

Dwell in glory as on an altar of your delights,
there let me offer you my sacrifices,
begging you to keep far from me the arch-enemy.
Grant me the grace to radiate your love.

Poet - Theologian / Ruanda

SARVADHARMAN PARITYAJYA
Mam ekam sharnam vraja
Aham tvām sarvapāpēbhyo
Mōkshayishyāmi ma shuchah

"Give up all things of law.
Turn to Me, thine only refuge,
(For) I will deliver thee
From all evils; have no care".

(Bhagavadgita, XVIII, 66)*

In Thine shelter are we all, O God,
without Thee nothing holds this world.
Alas, the religions which should show us the right path
to Thee and to Thine world,
are befooling us in unworthy things,
and do not do what they are for.
They are still mad after converting others,
thinking they and theirs are the best.
My prayer to Thee is, O Lord,
to give us all the vision
to see all religions equally as Thy creation.
What matters if one names himself Hindu,
Muslim, Christian, Jaini or Buddhist?
What imports is that he is Thine
and follows sincerely Thy path.
Alas, still there is no worse enemy
of religion than religion,
what an Indian lamented fifty years ago.
My hearty prayer to Thee, O God,

---

* From "Hindu Scriptures" transl. by R. C. Zaehner, Everyman's
Library, pub. Dent 1966 and 1972

Give religious leaders a loving heart for Thy other
    names
and Thy Teachings.
Unless this is developed,
the inhuman act that has happened
in the Indian Subcontinent and Middle East,
in Ireland, in Cyprus and some African countries
will for ever repeat.
I pray Thee, O Lord, and pray Thee again
to lead us all into light
so that all religions may live in peace
and perhaps help each other for a better world,
and people on this earth be brethren
as we are all only Thy sons.

                                    **Chemist / India - Italy**

DEAR JESUS,
you know our needs.
We beg of you —
sanctify us through your Spirit
that we may see what you see in us.
In all the events of our lives
let us make our way towards you
and recognise the use you make of these lives.

Your gifts are so great
that our whole life has only to correspond
        with them
in time and in eternity.
We cannot possess your gifts,
but you possess us through them,
so that your will may be done by us.
Dear Jesus,
you are present here and now,
do not allow us to stray into the past
or to lose ourselves in the far distance.
Work through your Holy Spirit
that we may live out with you
in the present
what has been and what is to come.

Make us live wholly in your presence:
adore you and love you in thought and in deed.
Give to us a heart renewed
that we may see our fellowmen in your light
and recognise each one
not for what he does
but for what you have done for him.
Let us free ourselves from our narrow-mindedness
and acknowledge you as Lord and Saviour
of all men.

You belong to all of us —
even to those who turn away from you.
You are always there, ahead of us,
your grace prevails over all —
as redemption for those who welcome you,
as judgement for those who reject you.

Lord,
there are thick, dark clouds
covering my homeland.
Have pity on the people living there.
Grant that the witness to your Spirit
may burn in the hearts of those persecuted
and let your word penetrate the country like fire.

Even in direst need
you grant a fresh beginning.
In the deepest clefts you sow your seed —
it cleaves the rocks and reveals
your glory to us.

Do not allow us to confuse the real fruit with mere
    success.
Our deeds pass away.
You alone give the seed
and bring about its growth.
Jesus, take us into your service
and let us have some share in the growth of your
    seed
in time and in eternity.

Pastor / Lithuania - West Germany

SPIRIT OF THE FATHER AND THE SON,
Holy Spirit,
you who withdraw from me
when I reach out for you,
you who blow like the wind.
Torn and exploited,
with no knowledge of where to go,
I listen attentively
in a barren land,
a land formerly stirred by empty chatter and
ostentation.
You are as strong as fire and storm;
yet your fire does not destroy,
it purifies and brightens;
and your storm sweeps away only what is stale
and sickly
so that all that is fresh and healthy
may grow through your breath.

I find no name for you.
But even before I call to you,
you call within me.
Often I forget
that you dwell in me
where none can enter,
not even myself,
"where, with you as their source,
mysteries linger".
Often I wait
for an unmistakable message from you.
I should like to understand you,
to feel how you touch me,
how you renew the face of the earth,
transform its people
and their cruel, unhappy lives.

And you allow me to forget and wait,
and you do not cease to cry out in me
with sighs too deep for words.

Many a time I almost catch a glimpse of you:
when I can understand someone
or when someone understands me;
when someone comes to me
and gives me his hand
and takes his stand beside me.
When a quarrel is resolved,
when party factions begin to appear absurd,
when those no longer speaking to one another
once more find something to say,
prepared to overcome what divides them
by suffering together.
This exceeds man's powers,
here you are present.

Or someone, forgetful of self,
throws himself into the breach, risking his life,
because others are in danger.
He is not playing the hero,
he cannot do otherwise
because he is impelled from within.
Here you are at work,
reminding us in our hearts
that there is One
who came into the world
for this and for nothing else.
Darkness and evil surround us,
countless people
await in trepidation the next blow.
At the same time
someone accepts slights without hatred,

does his duty and more than his duty
cheerfully, generously, without counting the cost.
This exceeds man's powers.
Here gently, consolingly, you bring your fruit to
    maturity.

You have raised up prophets.
Down the ages we have had saints,
some vehement, some silent;
they were overshadowed by you.
They accepted God
and shone with your mysterious joy.
It is within your power
to create for us in our days
people such as these.
If only you will grant us faith
ready to listen, to be impatiently patient,
steadfast in our ups and downs,
in darkness and in twilight,
when we take scandal from the Church
or, with her, give scandal,
in the fragile weakness
of our hope and our feeble love.

Yes, grant us faith!
Then we shall no longer
be so petty
that we expect
to understand you.
In our utter ignorance
we shall realise
that you are in us
and give yourself to us
if only we let you
blow where you will.

Benedictine Nun / West Germany

## FATHER, HAVE MERCY

on my countless sins!
Hatred, resentment,
selfishness,
envy, sluggishness, indolence,
repeatedly beset me,
with all their petty meannesses,
depriving me of your presence.
But, Father, in spite of everything,
you have taught me to love,
even when my soul suffers a death agony.

Father,
I will accept unprotestingly
your holy will.
If you wish to take from me
what seemed to me of value,
I know
that you will give me, instead, greater holiness,
in greater poverty.
May you be praised, Father,
because, seeing my misery,
you deign to save me from it,
and you will
to count me among the number of your saints.

Father,
for so long you have nourished my soul,
you who know how to be silent and wait,
to bless and forgive.
Give me the strength now
to be able to maintain a dignified silence
and hope in your name,
now, when I shall be a prey
to mockery and intimidation.

Father,
make me strong when I am lonely and helpless.
Difficult days await me
and I must spend them
in earnest dialogue with you.
I am fearful, Father.
My soul is weak and I groan,
my actions cry out for justice.
Voluntarily excluded by those in power,
incapable of flattery,
in the silent truth of my conduct
I await the agonising decision
of those who detest me for no other reason
than the anger that your name engenders.

It would be so simple to seek help from the words:
"I will honour you
if you will fall at my feet and worship me"
    (cf. Mt 4:9)
Lord, what is a man worth
if he falls at the feet of another man?
He serves only as a laughing-stock,
and his name passes from mouth to mouth
with flattering hypocrisy.

I know you want me on my feet.
Before no one but you, Lord,
will I kneel in adoration,
only before you will I kneel,
for you raise me up
and lead me to the table of your banquet.
Father, I suffer torments for these people.
Forgive them!
Restrain your anger till you come.
You would not want me

to play a double game
with your holy name, would you?

So I will say:
Only one is my Father
and he is the one I obey.
Only one is my Brother
and he died on the cross
to reveal his love for us.
Only one is my Master,
the Holy Spirit,
who, since my baptism,
has made his dwelling in me.
I am a Christian:
my wealth is my poverty.
I glory only in my sufferings
while I try
to attune my conduct to the Father's will.

So be it since I am not alone.
My sole wish
during these years of affliction
has been to try
to radiate Christ
in my daily life.
This is the crime
for which they judge me.
My hope remains steadfast.

So be it then!
My holy patron saints
Catherine of Siena,
Stephen,
John the Baptist,
Ignatius of Antioch:

I looked to you
even before I could speak.
Strengthen me
with your joyful, encouraging presence!

Hard days await me
and I must spend them
in earnest dialogue with you
if I am not to weaken.
Praised be the name
and honour of my Lord.
Amen.

Educationalist - Poet / Chile

PRAISE BE TO YOU,
Lord of the world.
Your paths are straight.
Where do our paths lead?
You alone, O God,
can show us the straight path.
We must not deviate from this path;
if we do, we are lost.

What are we human beings?
Are we not as specks of dust in your kingdom?
Who sends us hither and thither?
Who knows where this or that speck is?
You alone know
whether we get somewhere,
or find a way
where we can catch a glimpse of life,
or whether we stay where we are,
and do not turn back.
You alone know this.

You alone know
where a speck of dust is carried.
Waves come and the wind blows,
and the speck of dust
that no longer rests in your hand
is wafted hither and thither.
It thinks itself big enough
to fashion the world
according to its judgement.
Nowadays man believes in the illusion
that he has to consider his earnings as all-important,
like the money-changers in your temple.
We are so insensitive
that we resemble

a vertical take-off plane,
seeing nothing but our own interests,
and we are blind to the destructive effects
on the world around us.
What has happened to our love for our neighbour?

Pollution is rife in the air, in the water
and on the earth.
Even human life in a mother's womb
is of no value.
Families are knowingly wrecked
for the sake of earthly gain.

Dear Lord,
man thinks only of today and tomorrow
and forgets
that in your sight
a thousand years are as an instant.
Even our earth, where many
have a hard struggle to earn their daily bread,
is as a speck of dust in your kingdom.
Lord, I beg of you
to saturate with your love
this particle of earth.
Merciful God,
plant in our hearts
something of your love.

Your love cannot be described
in words.
With all our knowledge
we merely come to a barrier.
You alone know,
and with your love we know,
what is beyond that barrier.

Merciful God,
help us to love one another
so that we have no desire
to knock our heads against a brick wall,
but rather, through your love, to find the straight
        path.
We beg of you,
have mercy on us.

Engineer / Egypt - Brazil

THANK YOU, LORD,
simply for the fact
that you exist,
that there is no room for you in our heads,
for they are much too logical;
we cannot fathom you
even with our hearts,
for they are too restless.
Thank you, Lord,
that you so near and yet so far,
and ever different,
that you are revealed and yet not revealed,
that we flee before you — to you,
and of ourselves we do nothing for you,
but, with your grace, everything,
that what I cannot understand
is yet never an illusion,
that you are silent . . .
We learned illiterates
are only cackling geese.

Priest / Poland

# O MY GOD

You have made my eyes dim
like those of Isaac in his old age.
I see the world as in a dark mirror.

Outlines become blurred,
making the distinction
between the faces of men
unimportant:
for in all of them your image shines through.
Landscapes sink into twilight
but they reflect
our eternal home.
My footsteps, now unsteady, sense your guiding
     hand —
in the hand of my helpers.

Will you show me an inner light?
O God, give me the strength
to go on learning your lesson to the very end,
in joyfulness, unwearied,
ever hoping for your light.
Do not abandon me when I grow tired,
grant me the patience I have not got
and give me the light of faith in your goodness,
for "in your light we see light".
Heal me, Lord,
then I too am healed;
for you give the light
and you create the darkness,
and you alone can say:
"Let there be light".
Amen.

Journalist - Teacher / Israel

HOLY SPIRIT,
I adore you.
Welcome to the tiny house of my life.
I praise you for feeling at home
even with me,
who am poor and weak.
Let your fire
take possession of me,
let your flames consume and purify me.

Holy Spirit,
take possession of my spirit,
of all my thoughts,
my imagination,
my will.
Strengthen the tiny flame
of my faith, my hope.
Holy Spirit,
take possession of my heart,
my feelings,
even those most deeply hidden.
Make of my frail heart
a temple of festive light.
Take possession, Holy Spirit,
of my body, my faculties and my strength.
Unite them in a harmonious hymn
of peace and love.
Yes, let Jesus become man
in this bit of the world
that is me.
Let his word strike root
in the shifting soil of my being.
Holy Spirit,
glorify the Father in me.
Let his will be done in me.

Make me daily bread
for my brothers and sisters,
permeated with the power of gentleness and
    forgiveness,
and strong with the salt of your love.
Yes, sanctify me to give Jesus to men.
Let his love
for the least and the poorest
be ever active.
Let me be his hands,
his heart and his word.

I praise and thank you,
life-giving Spirit,
source of all life in me,
giver of all that is heavenly.
May you be praised
for having, long ago,
begun your saving work in me.

Alleluia!
You grant my prayer.
Yes, you form me to be an active cell
in the communion of the Church of Jesus.
Bring this to fulfilment, Holy Spirit.

Alleluia!
You deign to grant my heart's desire,
born of a faith that hungers.
Do whatever you will.
I surrender myself to you
for the glory of the Father
and the happiness of my sisters and brothers.

Alleluia!
My thirst is quenched

for you are the spring of living water
in my tiny house.
Now all can come
because I can quench the thirst of each one
with a delicious, life-giving drink,
with you.
You penetrate the dry soil of my being,
the warmth of your nearness renews me.
In your light
I see all my brothers and sisters
with a fresh vision.

Alleluia!
Father, I adore you.
Jesus, I love you.
Holy Spirit, I belong to you.

Parish Priest / Belgium

## YOUR ANSWERS ARE SO SOFTLY SPOKEN,

Lord — and the world is so noisy,
all mill around in confusion —
their houses built on sand.
People fall unsuspectingly into the abyss,
yelling and screaming,
while restless monotony
causes many a heartache.
In this pandemonium
how can your signs
be understood today?

O Lord, I beg of you,
set these unhappy people free to see!
Your answers, Lord, are miracles
and the most wonderful truth.
Help us to give up our worthless spoils,
and give us, Lord, the grace of discernment.

Psychologist / West Germany

HOLY SPIRIT!
For us — you are somebody.
If you were not
you would never have enticed us
to enter into the shade of your silence,
to enter the enclosure.

Teach us now
how to go deep down
into this crevice
in the rock of the Church
where God's glory
is ever passing by.
But it is seen only from behind,
in the form of a servant,
only in your lowly dwelling
and only by eyes that see in a new way,
eyes truly poor.

You, the lowly dwelling of the Word,
come down and settle
in our slum —
our heart.

Like a network of light and truth
you brood over us
as densely as the night —
here, for better and for worse,
we are caught,
and, to our great surprise,
tried and tested
in your burning fire
as, day in, day out,
we die a slow death.

Holy Spirit,
all this happens
because for us you are somebody.
Because you are all in all
and you do, thank God,
whatever you will,
you who are one with the
Father and the Son,
for ever and ever.
Amen.

Benedictine Nun / Switzerland

"ALLAH IS THE LIGHT
of the heavens and the earth.
His light may be compared to a niche
that enshrines a lamp,
the lamp within a crystal
of star-like brilliance.
It is lit
from a blessed olive tree,
neither eastern
nor western.
Its very oil would almost shine forth,
though no fire touched it.
Light upon light;
Allah guides to His light
whom He will.
Allah coins metaphors for men.
He has knowledge of all things".[1]

Yes, Lord,
light of the heavens and the earth,
light upon light,
that is what you are!
You flood
every being
with your light,
and yet, Lord,
our world
stumbles
in deepest darkness
and does not find its way
to your light.
Exploitation, oppression,
persecution and terror,

[1] cf. The Koran, p. 217 (Penguin Classics)

H

poverty, sickness,
ignorance or fear,
industrial, social,
political crises,
helplessness, over-population,
environmental changes,
technical devices, loneliness —
ever-increasing darkness!

Is your light no longer there, Lord?
Or are we human beings
no longer capable
of receiving it?
Lord, do we really want
to see
your light?

Lord, you once
revealed yourself to us
on Mount Sinai.
Your light shone on Mount Sinai
and lit up with its blaze
the farthest corners
of the earth.
With their own eyes
people saw your light, Lord, and . . .
they soon turned
away from it
and turned towards
the calf
and adored it.
A molten, lifeless calf,
but it was the work
of their own hands!

And since that time, Lord,
they adore the work of their hands.

For:
"they were made
to drink the calf
into their very hearts".[2]
But a calf,
even a golden one,
cannot lead us
out of darkness,
for darkness
leads only to darkness!
Lord, only your light
can be light for us!

Only your light
can save us.
Therefore, Lord,
I call on you
and pray to you
as your faithful ones
prayed in the past.
"Allah does not charge
a soul
with more than it can bear.
It shall be requited
for whatever good and whatever evil
it has done.
Lord, do not be angry with us
if we forget or lapse into error.
Lord, do not lay on us

[2] The Koran, p. 342 (Penguin Classics)

the burden
You laid on those before us.
Lord, do not charge us
with more than we can bear.
Pardon us,
forgive us our sins,
and have mercy upon us.
You alone are our Protector".[3]

Doctor / Syria - Austria

[3] The Koran, p. 365 (Penguin Classics)

## OUT OF THE DEPTHS WE CRY TO YOU, O Lord!

Save our child from our misdeeds
and teach us once more the law
you wrote for our forefathers.

Deliver us from our false gods,
teach us to use your name aright
and to look to you for our peace.

Teach us to understand the wisdom of our fathers,
to honour their deeds
and to cherish the earth where they rest.

Teach us to safeguard the sanctity of life,
the inviolable right to growth and development,
the fulfilment of race and family.

Teach us to show respect for our neighbour,
in his body,
in the work of his hands,
and in his reputation.

Let us not grudge him the love of his wife,
the friendship of his neighbour
and the happiness of his home.

Teach us to discern our own happiness.
Let us, Lord,
love you above all others,
and see in our neighbour
not ourselves, but your own Son.

Diplomat - Writer / Finland

117

GOD, FATHER OF MY CHILDHOOD,
if you really exist
above us, in us and around us,
I should like to tell you something
about a child in Sweden,
a child who had no doubts
about your existence.
And I have many questions
to which I have been able to give
only my own answers.
Gladly would I listen in profound silence
to your answers.

The child was born
of deeply religious parents
who, although protestant,
were catholic
in their whole attitude towards their faith,
in their leanings towards mysticism
and towards the beauty of a liturgy full of
    symbolism.
It was infectious.
The child built altars,
often communed with her God,
at six years old wanted to be a nun
and was convinced
that the stars in the heavens at night
were holes in the golden halls of heaven
through which shone the celestial light —
holes made by the staff of God the Father
as he walked across the deep blue carpet of heaven.

Then came the persecution of the Jews,
concentration camps,
war, bombs over Hiroshima,

Vietnam and the tiger-cages.
The prayers that went up to heaven
from millions of tormented hearts
fell to the ground like stones
and by their sheer weight
stifled the beliefs of childhood.

One persecution
followed another,
one war another,
the oppressed became the oppressors.
Even in so-called times of peace
innocent people were torn to pieces by bombs
and from time to time earthquakes caused tens of
    thousands
to be sacrificed
and die in torments.
The priests said:
God's will is inscrutable,
but praised be his name for ever.
Amen.

The child,
now a grown woman,
living in Germany,
did not find her way back to the faith of the church.
Her road was a different one.
It led to the hospitals
where small mongoloid patients gurgled,
where hydrocephalic children were not allowed
    to die:
it led through the transit camps of the homeless
in the welfare state,
through prisons
where people were detained in solitary confinement

for long spells
until they were mentally broken:
it led her to the stinking cells
of men in dark dungeons
where those yielding power humiliated their
     fellow-men,
hounded them like animals,
in the name of the people,
and locked them up in prison.

And she waited for an outcry
from the priests,
at least from prison chaplains,
and expected a rebellion.
None came.
However, when a bishop
visited young prisoners in Berlin,
pious members of the Church
who, on their party flag,
misused the name of Christian,
left the Church in their hundreds.
Then the young woman reflected for a moment
whether she should come back.
But because she did not believe
in the statutes of this "club"
or in its sincerity,
she refrained from doing so.

The questions remained.
Almighty, all-knowing, benevolent?
How can these qualities be reconciled in a God?
Christ,
seated at God's right hand,
why did he rise from the dead
on the third day?

If Christ's life was eternal,
then surely he would be,
not in the kingdom of the blessed,
but among the damned in hell?
His place would be there.

A creator,
who,
in his almighty power and infinite knowledge,
created man,
knowing in advance
how weak and inadequate he was,
unable to help himself,
yet the creator condemned him?
A creator
who accepted reconciliation with man
only through the painful death on the cross
of his son,
yes, even sanctioned it and willed it?
Could a divine Father
not have forgiven
without demanding satisfaction?

Only a few of the questions.
But they sufficed
to make it clear to her
that this God was not her God.
And she created for herself
a different,
very untheological idea of God
by making a completely ungrammatical comparison
with the word "good":
Good.
Goodness.
God.

She no longer has a God of the bible,
a God of the catechism.
This God
whose name was stamped
on the buckles of the soldiers' belts
as they went into battle
to kill or be killed,
whose priests blessed
the weapons of both sides,
this God, in whose name
the crimes of the churches and of Christians
were committed;
as far as she is concerned,
this God is dead and buried
in the common grave.

But the longing for goodness and justice
of countless generations
of tormented people,
marking them
with the name of God and the gods,
this longing still lives on
indestructibly in her,
and goodness,
from which we are all still so far removed,
is her goal.

And only occasionally,
when she roams the country of her childhood,
among tall, silent trees,
and sees quite clearly the holes full of light
of his staff in the heavens at night —
she asks herself
if it was not after all God the Father
who, just for her sake, had hung up

the crescent of the moon
between silvery branches of withered pine . . .
And to this lost God of her childhood
she would like to put her questions
before the autumn storm
hurls the silver pine to the ground.

Social Worker - Writer / Sweden - West Germany

LORD,
they say I have been successful
and they point to the map.
They are right, the project has grown
and spread over the whole of Pakistan.
They say that from the desert of Makran,
across the slums of the big cities,
as far as the glaciers of Nanga Parhat,
leper patients in their huts,
villages and hamlets
are cared for, and provided with medicines,
and they are right.

Why then, O Lord,
am I sad at heart?

It is the same with your Church:
you have been successful,
the Church is established all over the world.
In the Punjab they sing the Mass in Punjabi,
in Kongani in Goan
and in Japan in Japanese.

But only you know
at what price this has been bought.

Judas.
You had him as one of your companions,
you shared with him your ideals,
you knew he was of the stuff
of which martyrs or criminals are made,
you did not give up,
you went on hoping,
you washed his feet.
And he betrayed you
with a kiss.

In this passionate,
holy, unholy friendship
he gambled away his soul.
John says that you went on your appointed way.
"The son of perdition" —
I don't believe it,
you couldn't do that,
no, you couldn't,
you couldn't . . .

Well I had to sacrifice Inayat
for the "bonum commune";
I signed the letter
so that the work might continue.
What will the young man do
when he has lost his job?
What remains for him
except to rely on his friends
— friends who advised him to sell his soul?
I know he let us down.
Order has to be maintained.
We have a job to do
and we cannot allow ten thousand patients
to suffer
because three people became involved in the social
    revolution
in the wrong way.
I know,
yes, I know.

But why did you tell us
to leave the ninety-nine in the wilderness
and go after the one that was lost
if you knew
that it could not be done?

Yet you speak so disdainfully of the ninety-nine,
of the just
who need no repentance,
the silent majority
who have their hopes too
and a right
to understanding on our part?

The one, the lost one —
and when one of the Twelve was lost
you went on your appointed way.
"The son of perdition" —
did you go after him?
How far?
If love sets limits,
is it still love?
You can't want me to betray love?
He did not expect this;
in spite of trade union hostility
he still believed in my love
and set no limits to it:
"She will never do it,
she won't",
and yet I had to sign the letter.
The one, the lost one,
and the ninety-nine others in the wilderness —

Lord,
I do not understand you.
How can I follow you
if I do not see the way?
Who are you?
Where are you?
What did you want to tell me
through this lost one

and through Judas whom you allowed to be lost?
To whom shall I turn
if not to you?
Who will understand my tears if you don't?
You, my brother,
you know the darkness,
you have endured it,
through it you were put to death
and you have conquered it.

Take me by the hand,
lead me in your ways,
through "the encircling gloom" into light.

Leprosy Doctor / West Germany - Pakistan

## BLESSED BE THE LIGHT,

that is your name, Lord.
We are formed
from the dust and from heavenly breath.
May we therefore use our eyes to find you
in our brother the beggar and in the flower,
in the worm and in the sea.
May all our five senses
be directed towards you,
unsullied by guilt and sin.
Guard our body
created in your image.
Nourish it with the sacred mystery
present in a drop of blood as in a crystal of ore.
Preserve our hands and feet
to follow the path of love.
Grant dignity to the vessels of clay
that we are,
so that we may help in your creation.

Pardon us, Lord, for the damage done
as we tread on the stones and plants of your kingdom.
They too will give you praise,
crushed though they be,
if you forgive us.
May evil be changed to good
in the footsteps of people of goodwill.

May your hand come down over the wood of the
    table,
once more make the sign
so that the wheat in our meal
may be sustenance from you.
Bless the nourishment
of the birds of the air,

of the tree in the ground,
of the stars in the sky surrounding you.
Bless the bread of the world.
Satisfy all hunger and thirst.
Console the anguish of the fleeting dust that we are!
If "each hour wounds us
and the last one kills us",
then we are dying a slow death.
But life belongs to you
and in you, eternal love, we rise again.

Father, give your spirit to our hands
as we work.
May all our labour, whether important or trifling,
be a brick for your temple.

For all living creatures we pray to you.
You have one heart, ready to welcome them all.
Bless those we love;
protect them from blame and repulsiveness.
We pray for the mother,
woman of joy and pain.
Forgive the sins of sons.
Give peace to the womb
which, at your heavenly word,
bore us into the world.

May the sick in their sufferings
hear your word.
Heal their bodies and souls,
that their pain may be a sacrificial offering to you.
Lord, you sustain the leaf in the wind.
Do not forget sickly children
who cannot know your designs.

129

I

Take to your heart those who suffer from loneliness.
May they listen to your silence
as a chorus in unison.

We pray to you
for our brothers and sisters
and for our enemies.
Give them bread and good health,
peace and joy,
to fulfil your holy law,
each going his own way,
with his own talents,
to complete your universal task.

The roads in this world are broad,
yet you are the only way.
May all travellers
find their bearings by your light!
Keep watch over every path,
shield from every abyss,
still the storms,
let water gush forth in the desert.
Let every wanderer arrive safe and sound,
and may you be one day
his final destination.

Have mercy on our misdeeds!
Those who have infringed your law
do not know what they have done.
May those languishing in prison,
whether guilty or innocent,
find in you their freedom!
May those in exile
find in you their home!
Emigrants plead earnestly before closed doors.

Caravans of sufferers traverse a deaf world.
Lord, since doors remain closed to them on earth,
give them, in your heart,
shelter and a sweet homestead,
you, O God, who are Love itself!

We pray to you
for lives just beginning.
If you care for a speck of dust
and for a star,
watch over these lives
which are coming alight.
Be mindful of mother and child
in this valley of tears.
May the eternal line of life
be noble and serene!

May every child refrain from killing,
may he work and pray.
May the world be filled with justice and peace
in the name of the Father and of the Son
and of the Holy Spirit.

We pray earnestly for the dying!
A body expires
and you want to gather to yourself
the fruits for all eternity.
May you harvest at that moment
with kindly hand
their final breath,
and in your mercy
may that life be transplanted
to abide in you.
And for the dead!
Offer your light to their closed eyes,

to a night without dawn!
You are the ocean of life.
To you all rivers flow back.
The shawl in the cradle,
the shroud in the grave:
give to this muted material
your eternal radiance
and sing to the dead their first song.
Merciful Lord,
give us your love.
Amen.

Poet / Bolivia

LORD,
because you are God
you became man,
and because you became man,
man can be man only
if he is divinised.

You became man
because you love your creation
and want to set it free.

Heavenly King, Comforter,
Spirit of truth,
present everywhere and fulfilling all.
Keeper of our possessions
and leader of the chorus in our lives,
come and dwell in us,
in us and around us
make incarnate God present.

We make this petition of you
because we know
that without the Holy Spirit
there is no Christ
and without Christ
there is no Holy Spirit.

Therefore we pray to you
give us strength
to commit ourselves wholeheartedly
for suffering mankind in our times,
in the name of true solidarity
with all those
who seek peace
and call on God

for justice,
with all those
who are despised or oppressed,
with all those
who struggle
for the dignity of man,
and learn with all those
who experience
the tragedy of loneliness
and isolation.

All of this,
Christ, we ask of you,
not as bearers of your name in this world,
but as humble servants
of the mystery of your incarnation,
the mystery given to us to guide us.

Give us the strength
to adore this mystery
of God-made-man,
to understand it
in all its depth,
in all its dimensions,
to be able to see it
as a harmonious whole,
and not to acknowledge partial truths
which separate
the incarnation from the cross,
and the cross from the resurrection.

Let this mystery,
as John understands it,
take possession of us:
for "we have seen it

with our own eyes
and heard it with our own ears . . ."
making us bearers
of the Holy Spirit,
bearers of the Blessed Trinity,
bearers of the Church.

You have given us
the light of knowledge.
Let this light
shine brightly in us,
in our lives
and in our actions.

You have made us the gift
of true manhood
so that we may pray
to be formed
through your divinity.
Lead us
through your grace
to a fresh discovery
of the essential principle
of balance
between manhood
and divinity,
united
in one and the same person
of the God-man,
so that the event of your birth
may live on in us,
so that the whole of the human race on earth
may reach the goal of your incarnation:
holiness.

Theologian / Greece

YOU GO YOUR WAY
incomprehensibly
past a mother's tears,
past a traitor,
past me.
As I cannot understand
your way,
let me at least be one of the two thieves.

You are relentless
in the choice of your instruments.
You decreed betrayal by one
who could not bear the consequences of his deed.

The role of mother
you give to the woman
whose great love makes it certain
that she can bear cruel suffering.
And to me as I go my way
you bequeath the image
of the mother of sorrows,
though you know that I haven't the strength
to draw the sword out of my heart.

I see you as God
treading a human path.
You know its meaning and its end.
You take up your cross
because you will to do so;
we do it only because we must.

Forgive me!
At each step I pray:
Grant that my cross

may have the meaning of your cross
and my life
the meaning of your death!

Theatre - Writer / West Germany

## LORD AND FATHER!
Your spoilt child
stands in your presence.
You have given me everything
that promises joy in life.
What I am saying to you
you have long known
but today I must tell you about it.

One day, like so many others,
I had to leave my native land.
God, you put me to the test.
I was lost,
I was unable to pray.
All was darkness and uncertainty.
You had patience, Father.
You waited.
Slowly I understood the value of suffering
and how fruitful it can be:
a fresh opportunity to understand others.

For the first time I found myself
among the weak and oppressed.
But I felt your hand on my shoulder,
I was not alone.
Thank you for the people
that I came to know,
those who helped me.
Thank you for the health of my children.
How much you have enriched
my present life!
I enjoy every ray of sunshine.
Listen to my prayer!
In this world,
where there is so much unhappiness,

I want to be a witness to your love
and to love others because I love you.

Look down on Portugal, my own country!
People from every race
whom we have brought to the faith!
They are without roots, without hope.
Tears and suffering
have become their daily bread.
Help us in our need!
Families and young people no longer find the way
to you.
We have to expect days of sadness.
Lord, do not forget my country!

Artist / Portugal - Spain

## FATHER IN HEAVEN

it is time you came.
For our time is running out
and our world is passing away.
You gave us our life with one another.
We have wrecked it by declaring war against one
    another.
You gave us trees and forests.
We have cut them down.
To the bird you gave the spring
and to the fish the rivers.
We have silenced spring and polluted the rivers.
To the work of your creation
you gave balance.
We have upset it and therefore come to grief.
Come, Creator of all,
renew the lifeless face of the earth.
Despite our unhappiness
give us hope for your Day
when, at peace with every creature,
we can laugh and praise you.

Jesus Christ, our Friend,
we cannot walk in your company
without our neighbours,
those near at hand and those far away,
friends and enemies.
Continue to be the friend of sinners,
poor with the poor,
weak with the weakly,
forsaken with those who are abandoned,
that they, and we with them, may have life.
We hope for the coming of your kingdom
as we hope for peace in this divided world.
We believe in your presence

just as we trust in meaningfulness,
even when faced with the meaninglessness of death.
We look for your coming
as we hunger for our daily bread.
Come, Lord Jesus, come quickly.

Holy Spirit, you are known to us
as power from on high,
as comforter in need.
We cry to you and our cry encourages us.
We call out to you and you call out with us.
We wait for you and you are in our hearts.
Open our eyes and we shall recognise
your footprints on our path.
Give us silence and we shall hear
your sighs in our prisons.
Take from us what you have to take
until we come to rest in you
and feel that we are resting,
aware of your life in us,
your burning love and your driving force,
your anguish and your happiness deep within us.
Come, Creator Spirit,
empty our heart of selfish anxiety,
fill our spirit with creative love.
Give us dreams and visions
of your kingdom of freedom.
Make us disconsolate if they are betrayed,
if they do not become a reality.

Father, Son and Holy Spirit.
The time has come, the time for the fulfilment of
    history,
the time for making all one with God and in God.

Theologian / West Germany

141

AS I WAS SITTING
at my desk tonight,
it suddenly dawned on me
that the peace
I had pursued for so long,
was at last with me.
My mind was at rest,
at least for a while.
I enjoyed deeply
this minute of respite,
surprised by the serenity
that so completely penetrated
my mind and body,
but also painfully aware
of its fragility and evanescence.

Recently I did experience,
now and then,
these moments
of unclouded tranquility,
during which
all my contradictions and worries
seemed to mingle
and end in a strange harmony.

From my heart emerged
a sweeping thankfulness to God
for all things as they are,
and for the beings whom I cherish.
For a moment I felt them so close
that it did seem to me
that I was literally touching
the stuff of life,
that I, they,
and the nature around us

form my life and Life itself.
My everyday life,
in its ridiculous simplicity
and dreariness,
became a modest offering
to the Lord of Life.
The inconsistencies
and uncertainty of living
ceased to harass my mind
and I became one with my life,
united
in an indelible, steady prayer
to God.

Philologist - Librarian / Vietnam - USA

HOLY SPIRIT OF GOD,
you are the Lord, the Life-giver.
In this we rejoice.
In you we rejoice.

Holy Spirit of God,
you are the Guide,
leading us to Jesus
who is the Way,
and teaching us of Him.

Holy Spirit of God,
you are fire,
sent to burn the dross,
to warm the cold,
to bend the rigid,
to unite the broken.

Holy Spirit of God,
you are wind,
sent to expel the stale,
to disperse the gloom,
to revive the dying,
to refresh the weary,
to renew the aged.

Holy Spirit of God,
you are the Paraclete,
given to stimulate,
to animate,
to enkindle thought and action.

Glory to God the Holy Spirit,
Lord and Life-Giver,
fire and wind,
Paraclete and power.

Glory to Him in His world,
        in His Church,
        in me, His child.
Glory. Glory. Glory.
        Amen.

Theologian / England

I COME BEFORE YOU, LORD,
to remain still
in the Eternal Presence
in the deep silence of Faith.
I close my eyes
to find you more easily.
But never shall my eyes be closed
in fear of seeing ugly sights
for always may my eyes
recognise your presence
in the world . . .

May I show my love
in action, not mere words.
Help me
to spread true love
in the world.
Grant that love
may penetrate
all peoples, all structures, all systems,
penetrating deep
into the very hearts of men . . .

May I love myself less and less
that I may love others more and more.
Help me to lose myself in love
in order to find myself in you.

Help me to speak out
when occasion demands
for speech is your gift, Lord,
and I have no right
to be quiet
through pride, cowardice or apathy.

Others have a right
to my words
for I have your message
to give them.

But my words must be true words
not hollow words or false words
or cowardly words
through which you cannot pass . . .

I am ashamed, Lord, I am afraid;
ashamed of my satisfaction
at my decent little life,
afraid of my little efforts
which I take for progress,
ashamed of what I give,
for it conceals what I withhold.
Strike, Lord, at the penury of my heart . . .

Help me to be filled with joyous and helpful toil,
to be alive
with gladness and bright hope.
Help me to give you everything
all the days of my life.
Help me to love you
with all my heart
and all my soul
and all my strength
for you are
Love and Life and Truth.

Educationalist / India

LORD,
help us
to know and trust and love you,
so to live and abide in you,
that all our prayers may rise up
and come before God
in you,
and that we may have
in you
the assurance that we are heard.

Lord Jesus,
increase our faith.
Help us to take time
to wait and worship
in the presence of God
until our faith takes in
all there is in our God for us.
For it is in prayer,
in the exercise of our faith,
waiting before the living God,
that our faith can increase,
and that we may see
the glory
of the Blessed Trinity.

There are so many things
on our hearts,
so many things we would ask for;
but help us to remember
that the friendship
and love of God
must be more to us
than the gifts we ask.

Help us to wait in silence
and give the Holy Spirit
place to breathe within us
His intercession
for those things
for which we have no words:
our longings
for peace in the world,
our distress
at the poverty,
the sickness, the hunger, the cruelty —
all those things
which have become part
of the pattern of our existence,
and which sicken the hearts
of all those who love you,
and, in loving you,
help us
to love our fellow-men.

In you
we glorify the Father,
and ask
that the Father may glorify you
by answering the prayers
which the Holy Spirit
breathes on our behalf.

Bishop / England

## AND ONE DAY
I unlearnt all the pious maxims.
And one day I learnt
that not everything is clear.

One day: I met the man
with the red turban as he was riding into the village;
quickly overtaking him on my horse
I greeted him with amusement
like some figure left over from a carnival.
I was silent when I next met him
at the "public health centre".
His deep head wound was being stitched
without any anaesthetic.
He sat upright on a stool
like a king, pale-faced, turban removed,
an emergency dressing at his feet . . .
I ran away and wept.
He had ridden for at least two hours
to endure this treatment —
at his feet the turban . . .

One day: I went up to "Mamita".
I questioned her:
she had sobbed bitterly throughout the evening
    devotions
in front of the tabernacle,
and only with great difficulty was she able to tell me
through her tears:
"My one and only chicken has run away from me".

One day: I sent home photos of Ponciano.
My friends,
amazed at such ragged clothes, said:
"She has dressed him like this on purpose".

One day: mothers were carrying their dead children
in cardboard boxes (obtained from trashy shops with
    great difficulty)
to the priest's house to be blessed
and then to the cemetery,
laughing youngsters accompanied them . . .

One day: barefooted South American Indians
stood in front of their huts
waving flags
to greet the first North American
who, as representative of the human race,
had been on the moon.

One day you had really touched me, Lord,
and I decided
never again to look as though I did not care.

Then I became intolerant —
aggressive against lack of understanding
and against apathetic sectarian Christianity.
I began to point my finger
at the guilty,
then I rebelled
against so much suffering and injustice
and wanted to do everything at once . . .

And today?
Lord, I still continue to think
that we have the means to act,
but at the same time I wait for Christmas,
since on that day a person will be born.
And I hate a child that is dead.
I complain of my fellowmen,
I accuse mankind,

151

because they do not move on from where they are.
And I don't see
that I am hitting out against the cross
— and passing judgement on myself —
For I can begin with your becoming man
and myself becoming human.
Every day.
But I hope, Lord,
in your Spirit,
that each day he may rouse me
and prevent me from going to sleep.
For, Lord, your mattresses
are hard.

Social Worker / West Germany - Bolivia

O LORD,
the burning sun sheds its rays over the mountains!
Yes, you created
noonday brightness
for you are indeed the noonday heat.

O Lord, you also created
the hours
when we hasten from one joy to another
and are filled with wonder,
you the unending, breath-taking hour.

O Lord, it was you who created
happiness and sadness mirrored in human eyes.
When they look at me I know
that you, the incomprehensible God, see me.

O Lord, you decreed too
that nightfall should come upon the world.
Then we yearn for your eternity.
And no one knows where the stars end.

Theologian / West Germany

## LORD, WE WOMEN
have little reason
to be satisfied and happy
with the way things are nowadays.

We not only share
the anxiety and disquiet of all
but are especially concerned
with the lack of love
and the restrictions on our freedom.

All too often
we are tools and victims
of economical, social and political selfishness,
within the family
and on national and international levels.

We love a life of beauty and purity
but we are suffocated by the flames
of a pleasure-seeking life.

We want to love one another in peace
but are stimulated to every kind of hatred,
abuse, and even crime.

We are sensitive to our role
as bearers of life
but have to bow to laws
that spell murder.

We are small and weak,
"the little flock"
of which, Lord, you speak
in the gospel.

Yet we do try
fearlessly to raise our voice,
to bear witness by our lives,
to be active with the means available
— means usually inadequate —
in order that justice,
freedom and love may increase in our midst.

Humanly speaking
our voice is small and weak,
but relying, God, on your power,
we shall be
an irresistible and effective power.
This we firmly believe.
Mindful of the words of the Bible:
"Woe to the man",
we try to be united:
in the parish, in the city,
in the province, in the country.
We are conscious
that sisterly support
is not only a source of increasing richness,
but also one of indomitable strength.

We praise you, Lord,
and we thank you
for what you allow us to do
each day.
The seed is tiny,
but, scattered in your name,
it will bring forth abundant fruit
for a better world.

Educational Adviser / Italy

LORD, WHAT IS YOUR LOCK-UP TIME?
Can you tell me?
What is your measure, Lord?
for contact, for play?
Here they tell us to fear.
They advise us to curse.
How odd, Lord!

Down here 4 p.m. is lock-up.
Man, goats, cow and soul.
10 a.m. is unlock.
Man, goats, cow and soul.
We reserve the nights for weeping,
the day to entertain grinning and fear.
How odd, Lord!

O world, O landscape, O beauty,
what shall I share with you?
O hollow beauty of my soul,
my kith and kin
I loved, with problems shared.
O soothing, how easy — my soul to rest.
Today I fret my soul in despair;
was it your intention, Lord?

Shall I pity you, O village?
With your genial suicide lost,
your patience drained,
you've turned against son and daughter,
what then is your worth?
Is there any man
left to trust in your confines?
Nobody, Lord, just nobody.
Even you, Lord,

you seem so far,
so much aloof, unconcerned.

Shame upon us!
We have betrayed our character, hospitality,
we cannot live to face ourselves.
O Bullet, you are reigning indeed.
Come, Lord,
we want to count on you.
They tell us
you never let anyone down,
always on stand by,
always re-assuring.

But, Lord,
we love our children,
they are dear to us,
they are our hope, our life and our survival.

Our sons and daughters have left us
without a warning,
without a goodbye kiss.
They have left, Lord.
From schools, playing grounds and backyard.
For what? Death!
Why do they stay back?
What's funny in another's death,
Lord of a child?
Can you tell us why they left?
You are supposed to know,
They say you truly know.
Please tell us, Lord.

I wake up with a blank face,
they tell me I am content.

I smile at myself.
They like to think I am happy,
they drive me and I turn my back on them.
They hail it obedience.

Lord, they have what they want,
they are content.
They have money, fame, glamour.
But, Lord, do they feel as I do?

I always feel a vague discomfort,
an indefinable unhappiness,
Lord, they have fenced in my soul.

Some of us live in protected villages,
a fence and men around us:
a symbol of fear,
shadows of hate,
edifices of insecurity.

Some of us move in cities,
places of work.
Sunset comes,
we pile up in bus
to our locations.
They frighten us,
they haunt us.
Our children have disappeared
from those dark lanes.
Will I find my Tsitsi[1] at home, Lord?
My heart throbs,
throbs hard.

In fear, in confuson,
I walk back home,

a stranger at my door
asking awkward questions about my Temba.[2]
Anyway, Lord, you know the rest.
When you created me
you knew what you were doing.
I don't question your wisdom.
But I am worried about your slowness.
Night is a terrible time for me.
A vigil in tears,
dawn, well, a time of sounding my fears.

Priest / Zimbabwe

[1] Tsitsi (mercy)
[2] Temba (special friendships)

MARTIN HAS GONE.
Once more I encouraged him and gave him good
    advice,
peacefully, objectively, sympathetically.
He said it was helpful
when I talked to him in this way.
Only now, alone in the silence of my room,
do I realise
that inside me things are very different:
upset and agitated,
I no longer know
what to think;
I can't help him
and I feel helpless myself.


Tomorrow he will begin
a long prison sentence,
intended to teach him
how to live a well-ordered life in the future.
He won't learn any more
than he did during his previous detention.
To be good,
he must be able to experience goodness,
love, understanding, trust and respect;
instead he is going to experience all the things
that tormented him in childhood
and proved an obstacle to kindness and goodness
    in him:
rejection, humiliation, and coldness.
Lord, I often wonder
if I have understood
your message correctly.
Of all that I learnt
in earlier life
above all I gathered:

that we should love our neighbour,
and that it is our duty
to go out to the least of your brethren,
to do for them
what we would gladly do for you.

And as a child
when I learnt the tragic story of your life
how gladly I would have done all this:
I would have stood by you
when others abandoned you,
I would have watched with you,
defended you
when people mocked you with angry words,
and if I could have managed it,
with all the strength of my arms
I would have wrenched the instruments of torture
from your tormentors,
driven them off and freed you from suffering the
      imprisonment
inflicted on you because of your message.
I would have gone with you
to live your simple life,
gone with you on foot in all your ways
to search out human beings.
Despite sneering looks I would have spoken kindly
to Mary Magdalen
and how gladly — I must admit —
I would have severely reprimanded
the Pharisees and Scribes.

At that time I didn't know
that all these dreadful things
still happen a hundred times over
to human beings,

and I still feel the same despairing sadness
that I am too weak
to prevent all these horrors.

Now I know, Lord,
where to find the least of your brethren:
in slums all over the world,
in prisons,
in orphanages, in areas of catastrophe,
in the frightful slaughter of wars
you are present in the people of both sides,
it is you who bleed to death, crying out,
failing to see any meaning in it all,
in the indescribable distress
of ill-treated children
and tortured prisoners,
in old people who have been abandoned.

There your Spirit still breathes in vain.
Plead louder, admonish with greater insistence.
Express yourself more clearly.
Give us words and ways
of helping to make your message come alive,
your message of love,
pardon and respect for our neighbour,
of responsibility for one another.

Have I rightly understood
that this is the most important part of your
      message?
Then let me — over and above my own happiness —
not forget your instructions,
and in everything
that makes my life so wonderful,
let me find strength to pass on your love to others.

Lecturer in Social Studies / West Germany

LORD,
Do you know Barbara?
The foreigner
who did not know her own father,
does not know her own name
and cannot speak her own mother tongue?
She was carried away
from Russia by the German army
because she had fair hair and white skin,
and she was only eight years old.

She remained a foreigner.
She learnt German
and forgot her mother tongue.
In the German church services
she found an echo of her childhood,
a reminder of the incense,
priests and icons of Russian monasteries.
She became a primary school teacher,
married a German pastor,
bore him three children
and now has her own house.

But she remained a foreigner.
Her children learnt from friends
the songs sung by young people,
catchwords of Marx, Lenin and Mao,
an echo of the revolutionary jargon of her childhood,
a reminder of red flags and processions.
In her homeland she is a stranger.
She is a stranger to the foreigner.
She is a foreigner to her own children.

Lord,
you are a God of foreigners,

your Son came into a foreign land,
so that a foreign land might become home for us.
Are you a home for Barbara,
the foreigner,
or are we her home?

Theologian / Switzerland - England

YOU LOOK ON MAN
as no other man looks on him.
You know the good
that is done spontaneously,
the love
which unobtrusively upholds this world,
tenderly cherishing
the tongue-tied mortals that we are.
You hear the silent prayer
underlying the words
we say to you.

Once you looked on us
as men of the future.
It was thus that we stood before you,
side by side,
upright, mature,
no longer subject to anyone.
You created us,
intending perfection as our goal,
you attuned us to your voice
and I became myself;
without a trace of condescension
you became our Father.

And ever since then,
up to this day,
you have told us
to do whatever is right,
whatever is good,
to shield one another
from destitution and death;
to love the stranger
who stays awhile in our midst.
Darkness has not overcome

the Word you implanted in us
from the beginning
as a living heart
— the darkness did not overcome it.

The voices of prophets
have brought us your words,
they have called out to us,
telling us who we are:
for what purpose we exist,
for whom,
for you:
and our conscience was roused to new life,
it became water from the rock.
And when we had to pass
through the valley of death
and no longer knew the way —
you gave us
your well-beloved Son.

Never did man speak like this man.
In him we understood
the meaning of our life,
your reason for creating the universe,
the deepest abyss
and the highest heaven.
When your name
— as happens now too —
was profaned,
and when in time our cries of despair
reached their climax
so that our birth seemed in vain
— then he came,
he who was your Word,
who accomplished all justice,

who was for all of us the bread
that nourishes the world,
a cup of water
given to the least of his brethren;
he who raised the dead,
who as one before his time
broke through the curse of our night,
we saw him with our own eyes . . .
— he can never die again.

We
who, with all mortals in our world,
also die,
we
who, with all those who are still alive,
live for the day of your coming,
when,
clad in light,
with veiled eyes,
we shall see you,
see that you are all in all;
ever further removed
from that place we long to reach,
blind to one another,
weary unto death we call to you.

We ask you
why the charred remains of our dead
are blown away,
why the poorest on this earth
are mercilessly crushed;
why we,
with only a few others,
possess what belongs to many.
We hear your word, it is true,

but we do not understand it in practice.
Why do we know clearly
what life means,
and yet fail to live it?

You promised us
that we should be your breath,
your strength in this world.
Arouse our strength,
deaden our passions,
so that,
supporting one another,
we may, as one in you, persevere to the end.
Console us here and now,
give us a fellow-helper,
take us by the hand.
You know only too well
how often we give up hope.

You
who know us,
who penetrate beyond our outward appearance,
who seek us
where we are still humble,
gentle, good and steadfast,
— from this point,
at this moment in our lives,
we make our way forward towards you.
Because you urge us to go,
because you are the light,
invincible God,
let your name and your peace
shine upon us.

Writer / Holland

GOD,
I wake up
as heavy as lead
my limbs weary
my heart dull
my mind apathetic.

God,
I must take upon myself —
this daily battle with time
time of paralysing pressure
time of organisation and trifles
time of recalcitrant machinery
time of surfeit and of hunger
time of a show of anguish
time of extremes and terror
time of apathy
time of settling with the powers that be
a time blocked and clogged.

God,
Spirit of silence
Spirit of inflowing life
Spirit of glowing light
Spirit of returning strength
Spirit of loving truth
Spirit of sheltering love
Spirit of wholeness
Spirit of hope
Living water
Holy Spirit
Thank you.

Minister / Switzerland

LORD,
words fail me
to tell you all
I feel, I think,
and would like to ask you for.
Just as I am and in whatever way I speak to you
I know that you will understand me,
for you alone are Father of us all
and you lend your ear to the poor
just as readily as to the rich,
to adults as to children.

Lord,
although you already know
what I am going to say to you and ask you for,
I will put it into words.
I am making myself spokesman
for my brethren, all the American Indians,
they know what they need,
even if they cannot put it into words.

Lord,
thank you
for the fact that I have woken up today
hale and hearty,
with the hope of living
and of experiencing
the joys and sorrows
of my fellow-men.

Lord,
thank you for the rain, the sun and the fresh air,
which ripen the crops,
for the night full of stars
which makes us wonder

and think of your greatness,
for the flower, the birds and the sky —
for all that brings us joy;
for those who devote themselves
to teach us to read and write,
so that we may
live better lives
and learn your word,
for the moments
when I have received an open, sincere smile
from one of my brethren.

Lord,
I pray for that sick neighbour,
that she may not have to leave her children
        uncared for,
for that man's health
that he may be able to continue to work,
for his children,
for that worker
who toils tirelessly,
for the man with a stubborn heart,
that he may eventually let justice prevail,
for strength for our manager
to understand
how to act for the common good,
for that drunkard
to give up drinking
and once more lead a well-ordered life.

Lord Jesus Christ,
you well know all our needs
and problems.
Lord,
please give us the help

that you alone can give!
Teach us to understand
the meaning of suffering,
and give us the strength
to live for you
in the place which you have chosen for us.
Amen.

Farmer / Bolivia

## LET US AWAKEN, LIFT UP OUR HEARTS AND OPEN THEM WIDE!

Let us give thanks to the One who sets us free!
Let us be condemned
in the all-embracing unity of the cross
where the rebel slave dies
in order to share life fully
with all who are oppressed.

Nothing is more fulfilling
and nothing is more urgent
than to blend, to entwine the paths of our lives,
(carried away by the mighty wind of history),
united in harmonious thanksgiving
for you, the one and only Word,
for ever Son of man,
sprung from our earth,
formed of our flesh,
Jesus Christ.

You, in whom nothing is set apart,
nothing preserved, nothing safeguarded,
You, in whom all is given
and placed at the disposal of all,
You, who are the very gesture of sharing,
we call upon you,
we proclaim you,
we pray to you.

We are one with all of which we form an integral
        part.
The bread and wine are the fruits of human labour,
the bread bears within itself a fundamental need to
        be food for all,
and for each one;
the least hunger shatters the fellowship of mankind.

The wine, red, purple, is made for filling cups
on the family table of the assembled nations.
The bread eaten, the wine drunk by those who
	produce them,
become the body and blood of man to the very end,
humanity's flower and ideal,
the Son of man.

With the whole multitude of those alive
let us proclaim with one voice the Good News:
the truth of God's loving purpose,
that you hide from the wise, the calculating, the
	prudent
and the all-powerful,
to reveal it, to show it clearly,
to the poor, faceless, beyond counting,
the outcasts of the earth.

You are here present,
it is to you that we speak,
we celebrate your suffering love,
your love unto death,
a love which rebounds beyond death;
we make your passion
actual in our situations
of famine, distress, struggle, liberation.
Your conquering love becomes
a passion of resurrection.

Christ,
your invitation is for all those
who are thrust aside;
awaken us to our riches
as people risen from the dead.
We shall draw from your body and blood

the strength to labour passionately
to transform our lives and the whole of history,
to bring about the union of all
in one single nation,
the harmony of heaven and earth,
from north to south, from east to west.

May we all, as human beings, as the universe,
be ONE,
as you, Father, are ONE,
you who raise up the poor,
with your Word,
Jesus Christ,
the one united to the other
in your mighty common Breath.

Dominican / France

BREATH OF THE SPIRIT,
over the dread mountain —
icy wilderness —
where the dark forest portends death,
yet rose-coloured dawn
proclaims life.


Whisper scarce heard,
Comforter, be with me!
Be the sap rising
from the very roots of my being,
breath of my breath,
joy
in the heart of my pain,
bringing
day after day
the sun's pale gleam.


Holy Spirit, Comforter!
Pillar of fire!
Urging your puny creature's faltering steps
forwards, onwards!
You say:
shake off your sluggishness and shame,
climb the mountains
where lofty peaks await you.


Courage!
Renew your energy
at the mysterious spring.
See: already
earth is shrouded,
the heavens bend low —

a passing whirlwind,
and what is Mine will be yours,
for the Infinite,
yes, the Infinite, is close at hand.

Artist - Writer / Brazil - France

LORD JESUS CHRIST,
God's only-begotten Son,
I adore you, I confess
that you came from the Father
that we might enjoy eternal life with him.
Lord Jesus, I thank you
for giving me faith in you
and for giving me
the Holy Spirit,
Spirit of the Father
and your Spirit.

I beg of you to grant this faith
to all who are dear to me,
to all whom I meet along my path,
to all my fellow-countrymen, to all people.

I beg of you
to renew your Church
through the Holy Spirit
and to gather together
all the scattered children of God.

I beg of you
to reveal your glory through us,
that the world may see
that you are the Lord
and freely submit to your gentle lordship,
a lordship of justice.

In your name we pray:
Father, may your kingdom come!
May your name be glorified!

Come, Lord Jesus, come!

Theologian / Denmark

MERCIFUL FATHER,
almighty God, hear my prayer!
You who created
matter, life and understanding,
who are eternal and infinite,
know at each instant
what all your creatures
are thinking, feeling and doing!
Lord, hear my prayer!

For you said:
Ask, and you will receive,
for you, wholly love,
have created
goodness, beauty, happiness and health,
for you are pardon and hope!

Lord, hear my prayer!
Grant to my feeble faith
life and growth,
grant me enlightenment,
reflecting your Holy Spirit,
grant me the strength
not to be dragged along
by overpowering materialism
and not to be swept away
by the atrocious egoism
of civilised man.

Let my heart
become sensitive once more.
Let me really
see other people as my brothers.
Let pride, falsehood, covetousness and extravagance
disappear in me!

Make me grow in understanding,
that I may have a deeper sympathy with others;
make me grow in tenderness
that I may have a greater love for others;
make me grow in sensitivity
that I may never again be unjust!

Strengthen my competence
so that I may be of use to mankind!
Strengthen my imagination
so that my work may be creative and fruitful!
Strengthen my weak will
so that I may repudiate sin!

Do not allow me
to forget my past,
may the remembrance of it
safeguard me from blunders!
Do not allow me in future
to be blinded by flattery and pride!
Do not allow me,
even for an instant,
to be ungrateful and to forget you!

So I pray to you,
Father of all!
I pray for myself
and for every individual person,
so that the world you have created may become
        better,
that hatred, envy, lies and violence
may disappear from it once and for all!
And so may this world too
become part of your glory!
Lord, hear my prayer!

For my country
where, despite its long Christian tradition,
your grace is urgently needed
at this very grave moment in its history:
may the tragic experience
through which we are living
help us
to live together as brothers!
Lord, you alone can help us!
In your name we bear our faith
into the world.
In your name, now too,
let us find our way.
Amen.

Commercial Agent / Spain

## BECAUSE I DO NOT KNOW THE WAY
because you have said "I am the Way"
because the way is obscured by a thousand detours,
wrong signs, deceiving signs.
Each of them marked "One and Only"
because with all my intemperate heart
I want to arrive here and now
but must go on; to there, to then
because of duty and law and responsibility
and obligation and so on and so on;
how I weary myself (and undoubtedly you)
and lose your gracious gesture,
and tie myself in knots
because 'law' is a cover for my lawlessness,
not the freedom you offer,
and 'duty' goes along with my deviousness
and 'obligation' is hand in glove with my laxity
and 'responsibility' is a cover for childishness.
So I carry about these heavy absurd words,
a beast's burden
because in fact I wish to be burdened,
dread to be free,
which is to say, I dread to be your friend and brother.
Nevertheless
now and again your word reaches me.
What moments those are!
Everything stops short, as between heartbeats.
A strange joy, as though my face were touched
and held by two hands,
as though an egg split in two and I stood there,
born for a change; alive for a change,
utterly changed (for a change).
Then of course my old demons return;
or as they say, life goes on,
which is to say, and closer to the fact,

death goes on
except that death does not quite go on,
not in the old way,
not altogether calling the plays.
Those moments of grace!
Like an arrow of sunlight
along a mausoleum floor.
Something is happening,
the door must be slightly ajar.
I have a name for you;
you are the crack of light
under the door of the city morgue.
Any minute now I may hear my name called:
'Lazarus'!

Jesuit - Poet / USA

*Adler, Elisabeth,* born 1926 in Magdeburg, Germany. Studied Germanistics and History. Directress of the Evangelical Academy in Berlin-Brandenburg, East Germany.

*Altwegg, Magdalena,* born 1924 in Wädenswil, Switzerland. School of Commerce. Instructor as medical laboratory assistant. Ten years' professional work. *Abitur* at evening classes. Studied Evangelical Theology. Parish minister in Adliswil, near Zurich, Switzerland.

*Austin-Trinh, Christane,* born 1943 in Hué, South Vietnam. Education in Vietnam and France. College and University studies in USA. Married to a German professor of Germanistics. Lives in USA. Lecturer, teacher, librarian.

*Bamberg, Corona,* born 1921 in Fürth. Studied Philosophy, Philology, Germanistics and History. Doctor of Philosophy. Since 1947 Benedictine nun in Holy Cross Abbey, Herstelle, Germany.

*Bedregal, Yolanthe,* born 1916 in La Paz, Bolivia. Studied at the Academia de Bellas Artes in La Paz and at Barnard College, Columbia University, New York. Subsequently lecturer in Aesthetics and History of Art at the College of Education in Sucre. Temporary Secretary-General of the PEN-Club in Bolivia. Vice-President of the Ateneo de Bolivia and member of other cultural institutions. Contributor to several periodicals. For her services in cultural circles she has won the title of honour of "Yolanda de Bolivia". Most famous poet in her country. Editor of several books on poetry, art and education. Married and living in La Paz.

*Ben-Chorin, Schalom,* born 1913 in Munich, Germany. Studied Philosophy, Germanistics and Comparative Religions. Has worked since 1935 as journalist, writer and lecturer in Jerusalem. Married, father of two children.

*Berrigan, Daniel,* born 1921 in Syracuse, New York. 1931 entered Society of Jesus. Studied Philology and Theology in USA. Prize-winning poet. Well-known for his appearance with eight friends in Catonsville during the Vietnamese war. Burning of conscription papers with home-made napalm purloined by the group from the War Office. Court case leading to imprisonment. Now works as a Jesuit in New York.

*Blois de, Lieselotte, Countess,* born 1937 in Vienna. Studied Philosophy, History of Spirituality and Culture in Vienna, Cambridge, Oxford and Paris (Sorbonne). Doctor of Philosophy. Lectured at University of Vienna and in Salzburg. Since 1970 married and living in Johannesburg, South Africa. Mother of two daughters.

*Brohi, A. K.,* born 1918. President of the Bar Association in Pakistan. One of the leading lawyers in his country. Temporary Government Minister of Justice. Leading author of the first Pakistan constitution. Very active in politics. Adviser to the Government. Married. Three children.

*Càmara Alvarez de la, Luis Maria,* born 1912 in Barcelona. Attended a school of building. Commerce. Active in an advertising firm. Agency for foreign investments. Married. No children.

*Cardonnel, Jean,* born 1921 in Figeac, France. Dominican Friar. Works as a chaplain, especially in social work. Writer. Well-known for his activity for a contemporary form of life for priests. Lives in Montpellier.

*Clark, Alan,* born 1919 in Bickley, Kent. Studied at Westminster Choir School and English College, Rome. Ordained in 1945. Since 1969 Catholic Bishop of East Anglia. Lives in Norwich, Norfolk.

*Coggan, Donald,* born 1909 in London. Studied at St John's College, Cambridge, and Wycliff Hall, Oxford. 1931/34 Assistant Professor for Semitic Languages and Literature at Manchester University. 1934 parish priest at St Mary's Church, Islington. Professor of New Testament at Wycliff College, Toronto, Canada. 1944 returned to England. Worked in theological college, London. 1956 Bishop of Bradford. 1961 Archbishop of York. 1975/79 Archbishop of Canterbury, Primate of the Anglican Church in England. Married in 1935. Father of two daughters.

*Cremar, Drutmar,* born 1930, in Coblence, Germany. Secondary School studies at Jesuit College, Bad Godesberg, leading to *Abitur* in 1952. Entered Benedictine Abbey of Maria Laach. Studied Philosophy there and Theology at Beuron, Hohenzollern. 1958 ordained priest. Youth chaplain and other duties. Since 1971 in charge of the Art workshops and publishing firm in Maria Laach.

*Dalrymple, John,* born 1928 in North Berwick, Scotland. Secondary school studies at Benedictine Abbey, Ampleforth. Theological studies at Gregorian University, Rome. Works today as a parish priest and writer in Edinburgh, Scotland.

*Dammert Bellido, Jose,* born 1917 in Lima, Peru. Studied Theology. Doctor of Law. Ordained priest. Now Bishop of Cajamarca, Peru.

*Domin, Hilde,* born 1912 in Cologne. Studied Jurisprudence, National Economics and Sociology. Student of K. Jaspers and K. Mannheim. Dr rer. pol. in Florence 1935. Teacher and University lecturer in England and Latin America. Translator, photographer, writer, poet. Won Rilke prize in 1976. Married. Lives in Heidelberg.

185

*Eggeborn, Ylva,* born 1950 in Stockholm. Studied Literary Criticism and Theology. Journalist and poet. Married. Mother of one daughter. Lives near Stockholm.

*Friedjung, Bruno Eliahu,* born 1908 in Vienna. Technical schools. Has lived in Israel since 1934. Qualified engineer. Town planning. Married. Father of one child.

*Harun, Helmut,* born 1914 in Westhoven/Rhineland. Theatre. Writer. Has won various literary prizes. Lives in Duppach near Gerolstein/Eifel.

*Hemmerle, Klaus,* born 1929 in Freiburg in Breslau. Studied Theology. Doctorate in Theology. 1952 ordained priest. 1956/61 Director of the Catholic Academy in Freiburg. 1968/74 Spiritual Director of the Central Committee for German Catholics. 1970 Professor of Fundamental Theology in Bochum. 1973 Professor of the Christian Philosophy of Religion in Freiburg. 1975 Honorary Professor of the University of Freiburg. Since 1975 Bishop of Aix-la-Chapelle.

*Hollenweger, Walter J.,* born 1927 in Antwerp. Banking. Studied Theology in Zurich and Basle. Doctor of Theology. At present Professor of Theology in Birmingham, England.

*Hygen, Johann Bernitz,* born 1911 in Oslo, Norway. Studied Lutheran Theology at Universities of Oslo, Berlin, Tübingen, Leipzig, Zurich and Oxford. Doctorate in Theology. Pastor in Oslo 1941/45. 1948 Professor in Philosophy of Religion and Ethics in Oslo University. Married. Father of three children.

*Illies, Joachim,* born 1925 in Ketzin, Havel. Studied Science. Professor of Biology in the University of Giessen and in charge of out-patients' department for Limnology at the Max-Planck Institute in Schlitz, Hessen. Married. Father of four children.

*Kagame, Alexis,* born 1912 in Kiyanza, Ruiza, Ruanda. Studied Philosophy and Theology at the seminary of Kabgayi, Ruanda. 1941 ordained priest. Degree at Gregorian University, Rome. Editor-in-chief of the periodical: "Kinya-Mateka". 1953 and 1954 journeys to Europe. Numerous articles on historical, folklore and theological topics.

*Korzenszky, Richard,* born 1941 in Csorna, Hungary. Studied Philosophy and Theology in Pannonhalma. Studied ancient Hungarian literature and Russian in Budapest. Ordained priest 1967. Now teaching at the Abbey High School in the Benedictine Abbey of Pannonhalma, Hungary.

*Krüger, Hildegard,* born 1940 in Asunción, Paraguay. Studied History at the University of Asunción. Degree at Cologne University. Doctor of Philosophy. Head of the Union of German Women in Cologne. Married. Two children.

*Lee, Ok-Bun,* born 1942 in Sunsangun, Keong-Buk, South Korea. High school studies. Trained in Germany as a nurse, social worker, educator. At present works as a tutor in Cologne.

*Lohfink, Gerhard,* born 1934 in Frankfurt. Studied Theology. 1971 Doctorate in Theology. 1973 Sabbatical year. Since 1976 regular Professor for New Testament at Tübingen University.

*Malinski, Mieczyslaw,* born 1923 in Brzostek near Cracow. Theological studies. 1949 Degree in Cracow. Philosophical studies. 1963 Degree in Lublin. 1967 Doctorate in Theology in Rome. Student under Karl Rahner. Now works as a chaplain in Cracow.

*Marti, Kurt,* born 1921 in Berne, Switzerland. Studied Evangelical Theology. Now pastor of the Nydegg parish in Berne. Writer and poet. Married. Father of four children.

*Meeuws, Jan,* born 1940 in Heerlerbaan, Province of Limburg, Holland. Entered with the de Montfort Fathers. Studied at Oirschot, North Brabant. 1967/68 probationary year as deacon at Boxtel. 1968 ordained priest. Parish priest in Louvain since 1968. Leader of a charismatic prayer group.

*Méndez Flores, Balbino,* born 1947 in Lavadero, Bolivia. Studied and trained as an agriculturist. Married. Three children.

*Messerschmidt, Lars,* born 1937 in Copenhagen. Studied Theology. Degree in Theology and Sacred Scripture. Parish priest of a Catholic parish in Copenhagen.

*Meves, Christa,* born 1925. Studied Germanistics, Geography and Philosophy at the Universities of Breslau and Kiel. State examination in Hamburg. Additional studies there in Psychology. Further psychological studies at the Psychotherapeutical Institutes of Hanover and Göttingen. Has her own practice in Uelzen. Married to a doctor. Mother of two children.

*Minwegen, Hiltrud,* born 1929 in Essen, Germany. Studied Philosophy and Germanistics. Degree. Married. Mother of three children. Wife of a German diplomat. Lives at present in Rome.

*Moltmann, Jürgen,* born 1926 in Hamburg. War experiences. Imprisonment. Studied Evangelical Theology. Professor of Evangelical Theology in Tübingen.

*Mveng, Engelbert,* born 1930 in Enam-Ngal, Cameroon. Entered Society of Jesus. Studied Philosophy and Theology at the Universities of Dekar (Senegal), Namur (Belgium), Lyons and Paris. Ordained priest. Professor of Theology at the University of Yaounde, Cameroon.

*Nunes Mexia de Castelo Branco, Maria da Graca,* born 1931 in Cascais, Portugal. Studied Philosophy and Fine Arts. Married. Mother of four children. Lives in Madrid.

*Oosterhuis, Huub,* born 1933 in Amsterdam. Studied Philosophy and Theology and Dutch Philology. Chaplain to students in Amsterdam and leader of the social and cultural centre "De Populier" in Amsterdam. Married. Two children.

*Ostbomk-Fischer, Elke,* born 1944 in Ybbs, Austria. High school studies. Vocational school for Kindergarten teacher. Taught for five years. Further education in Sociology. Graduated as teacher of Sociology. Directress of a home called "The Open Door". Married. Lives in Germany.

*Orientar, Anita,* born 1896 in Bahia, Brazil. Grew up in Germany. Doctorate in Philosophy. Became a painter. Lived in Paris and near Lake Garda, Brescia. 1933 Conversion to Catholicism. Worked as a teacher. 1939 emigrated with her parents to Rio de Janeiro. After the war moved to New York. 1962 returned to Germany. Now lives in Vence, near Nizza.

*Orzechowski, Christel,* born 1943 in Lyck, East Prussia. Trained as a kindergarten teacher. Studied Social Pedagogy. Spent three years in Bolivia helping with development work. At present has similar duties in the Andes, Peru.

*Pachmann, Ludek,* born 1924 in Bela pod Bezdezem, Czechoslovakia. Attended a technical school. Now journalist and writer. International chess player. Lives in Berlin. Married.

*Papandreou, Damaskinos,* born 1936 in Gato Chrysoritsa, Etolia, Greece. Studied Orthodox Theology in Halki and at the Universities of Bonn and Marburg. Doctorate in Theology in Athens. 1970 appointed Metropolitan of Iranoupolis. 1974 appointed Professor in the Theological Faculty in Lucerne, Director of the Orthodox Centre of the Ecumenical Patriarchate in Chambéry near Geneva. Liaison officer of the Commission "Faith and Order" of the World Council of Churches in Geneva.

*Peek-Horn, Margret,* born 1936 in Cologne, Germany. Studied Germanistics and Catholic Theology in Paderborn, Bonn, Munich and Innsbruck. Degree under Karl Rahner. Worked as an Assistant at the College of Education at Neuss in the Rhineland. Now a Lecturer in Theology. Married. Lives near Jülich.

*Pfau, Ruth,* born 1929 in Leipzig. Medical studies in Germany. Degree. Specialised in treatment of leprosy in India. Conversion to Catholicism. Member of the Congregation of the Daughters of the Heart of Mary. Since 1960 has worked with lepers in Pakistan. Care recently also of tubercular patients in Pakistan.

*Posada, Juan Rafael,* born 1947 in La Estrella, Columbia. 1963 entered the Claretian Order. 1964/71 studied Philosophy and Theology in Zipaquirá, Manizales and Bogota. Since 1969 has worked with various theatre groups in Bogota, Manizales and Medellin. Poet, dramatist. Won prize at the University of San Bonaventura, Bogota. Concerned with problems of mass media.

*Roscic, Nikola,* born 1940 in Grabovac, Croatia, Yugoslavia. Studied Philosophy and Catholic Theology in Zagreb and Rome. 1966 Degree in Theology in Rome. Lecturer in Fundamental Theology at St Bonaventure's, Rome. Member of the Franciscan Order (Conventuals). For some years Provincial of his Order in Zagreb. Now editor of the Catholic monthly periodical "Veritas".

*Rossi, Carmela,* born 1903 in Rovereto, Province of Trent. Studied Philosophy. Doctor of Philosophy at University of Milan. Teacher. 1946/49 chief representative of Catholic Youth in the Italian Catholic Action Group. 1959/67 representative in General Council for Italian Catholic Action.

*Rodrigues, Dulcinea,* born 1922 in Bombay, India. University studies. Married, five children. Active in many national and international spheres of political formation. Her interests and commitments are at the service of social-political and pedagogical projects.

*Ryan, Patrick,* born 1943 in Bronx, New York. Studied at Fordham University, New York. Further studies at Western-Michigan-University, Kalamazoo, Michigan. Since 1961 Trappist monk at the Abbey of Genesareth, Piffard, New York, USA.

*Schakfeh, Anas,* born 1943 in Hama, Syria. Studied Medicine in Vienna. Married.

*Shoukry, Baha Eldin,* born 1928 in Cairo, Egypt. University studies. Qualified engineer. Scientific assistant at the Technical High School at Aix-la-Chapelle. Consultant engineer for mineralogy in Germany, Italy, Finland, Algeria, Egypt and Turkey. At present leader of a project in Brazil.

*Shukla, Shyma Kant,* born 1928 in Marawat (Basti), India. Studies at the Universities of Benares, Rome and Paris. Degree in Paris. Chemist. Has lived for several years in Rome and works there as a research student at a national research Institute.

*Schellenberger, Bernardin,* born 1944 in Ellwanger/Jagst. 1963 *Abitur* and entry to the Franciscan Order. 1964/66 Theological studies in Munich. 1966 Transfer to the Trappist Order. 1968/72 Theological studies in France, Freiburg and Salzburg. 1972 Ordination. At present Prior and Novice Master in his abbey.

*Schneider, Severin,* born 1931 in Vienna. 1950 entered Benedictine Abbey of Seckau. Studied Philosophy and Theology. 1956 Ordination. Studied Philosophy and Germanistics in Graz. Doctorate in Philosophy. Now teacher at the Abbey School in Seckau, Obersteiermark, Austria.

*Stenius, Göran,* born 1909 in Wiborg, Finland. For many years chargé d'affaires of the Finnish Embassy to the Vatican. Novelist. After his conversion to Catholicism also wrote religious poetry. Married, with seven children.

*Tan-Friese, Siok-Hing,* born 1944 in Tegal, Central Java, Indonesia. *Abitur* in Cologne. Studied Old English and Germanistics at Cologne University. Studied Dentistry. Married to a qualified German economist. Lives in Düsseldorf.

*Troncoso, Mejia Eric,* born 1936 in Lautare, Chile. University studies in Santiago, Chile. Professor in Pedagogy and English at the University of Santiago. Poet, writer. Married, with two children.

*Le-Trung-Thanh, Josef,* born 1937, in Thai-Binh, North Vietnam. University studies in Nam-Dinh, Hongkong, Genoa, Rome and Paris. Ordained priest in 1959. Doctorate in Theology in 1974. Authorised episcopal representative in North Vietnam for all the affairs of his native diocese of Thai-Binh. Lives in Neuss/Rhineland.

*Twardowski, Jan,* born 1916 in Warsaw, Poland. Studied Polish Linguistics and obtained Master's Degree in this subject after the war. Had already decided to become a priest and was ordained in 1948. Worked for four years in a country parish. Since 1952 Rector of the church of the Visitation nuns.

*Urdze, Jazeps,* born 1909 in Gaudaizi, Lithuania. Studied Evangelical Theology. Evangelical pastor. Married, with six children. Lives in Germany.

*Walter, Silja,* born 1919 in Rickenbach, Olten, Switzerland. Studied Pedagogy. Teacher. Known as Sister M. Hedwig. Benedictine nun in Fahr Convent, near Zurich, Switzerland. Poet. Has published numerous works.

*Williams, Betty,* born 1943 in Belfast. Married, with two children. Founded, with Maired Corrigan, the Peace Movement for Women in Northern Ireland. Nobel Peace Prize in 1976.

*Wolf, Birgitta,* born 1913 in Helgesta, Sweden. Through her marriage came to Germany in 1933. Since 1954 has done welfare work, in an honorary capacity, for prisoners and their families. Awarded the Beccaria Silver Medal of the Germany Association for Criminology; Co-Foundress of the Action Society for criminal law and punishment reform. Freelance work for newspapers; lectures in criminology and punishment in Germany and elsewhere. Representative of the state-recognised organisation: "Help in Need, Birgitta Wolf, e.V.". Writer. Lives in Murnau (Upper Bavaria). Mother of four children.

*Wurmbrandt, Richard,* born 1909 in Bucharest, Rumania. Theological studies. Evangelical pastor. As such spent 14 years as Communist prisoner in Rumanian gaols. Many lively books about his shattering experiences during his years of suffering. Lives in USA.

The contributions to this anthology came from the following countries:

| | |
|---|---|
| Austria | Spain |
| Belgium | South Africa |
| Bolivia | South Korea |
| Brazil | South Vietnam |
| Cameroon | Sweden |
| Chile | Switzerland |
| Columbia | Syria |
| Czechoslovakia | Venezuela |
| Denmark | West Germany |
| East Germany | Yugoslavia |
| Egypt | Zimbabwe |
| England | |
| Finland | |
| France | |
| Greece | |
| Holland | |
| Hungary | |
| India | |
| Indonesia | |
| Israel | |
| Italy | |
| Lithuania | |
| Northern Ireland | |
| North Vietnam | |
| Norway | |
| Pakistan | |
| Paraguay | |
| Peru | |
| Poland | |
| Ruanda | |
| Rumania | |
| Scotland | |